DK First
FRENCH
Picture Dictionary
Canadian Edition

Contents

Project Editor Anna Harrison
Editors Elise See Tai,
Lucy Heaver
Editor, Canada Julia Roles
Project Art Editors
Ann Cannings, Emy Manby
DTP Designer David McDonald
Production Harriet Maxwell
Translator Chantal Lamarque
with Elise Bradbury

Managing Editor
Scarlett O'Hara

First Canadian Edition, 2005

Copyright © 2005 Dorling Kindersley Limited

Dorling Kindersley is represented in Canada by
Tourmaline Editions Inc.
662 King Street West, Suite 304
Toronto, Ontario M5V 1M7

Library and Archives Canada Cataloguing
in Publication.

DK First French picture dictionary.

ISBN-13: 978-1-55363-056-2
ISBN-10: 1-55363-056-4

1. Picture dictionaries, French. 2. French
language--Dictionaries, Juvenile--English.
3. Picture dictionaries, English. 4. English
language--Dictionaries, Juvenile--French.
I. Title: First French picture dictionary.

PC2629.D54 2005   j443'.21   C2005-900709-5

Colour reproduction by Colourscan, Singapore
Printed and bound in China by SNP Leefung
06 07 08 10 9 8 7 6 5 4 3 2

Discover more at
www.dk.com

How to use this dictionary

Find out how you can get the most from your dictionary. At the beginning of the book there are Topic pages. These include lots of useful words on a particular subject, such as *Pets* and *In the Park*. Each word has its translation and help on how to pronounce it. The words on the Topic pages can be found in the English A–Z and in the French A–Z. There are lots of other useful words here too. The verbs are in another section. At the back of the book there is a list of useful phrases for you to use when you practise your French with your friends.

Topic pages

topic heading

French entry word

French pronunciation

English translation

extra words on this subject

interesting fact

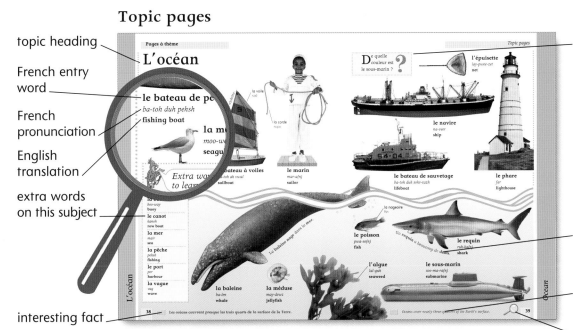

question for language practice

simple sentence with topic vocabulary

translation of interesting fact

English to French A–Z

first word on the page with the French translation

English entry word

French translation

French pronunciation

Look for me on the topic pages!

last word on the page with the French translation

this shows the first letter of the words on the page

Tout à mon sujet
All about me

*Je suis **grande**.*

le père
pair
father

la mère
mair
mother

Voici ma famille.

le bébé
bay-bay
baby

le grand-père
grandfather

la grand-mère
grandmother

la sœur
suhr
sister

le frère
frair
brother

les grands-parents
grah(n)-par-ah(n)
grandparents

l'enfant
lahn-fah(n)
child

*Nous sommes **contentes** !*

*Thomas est **en colère**.*

la tante
tahnt
aunt

l'oncle
lonk-luh
uncle

contente
kon-tahnt
happy

en colère
ah(n) ko-lehr
angry

Il y a environ 206 os dans ton corps !

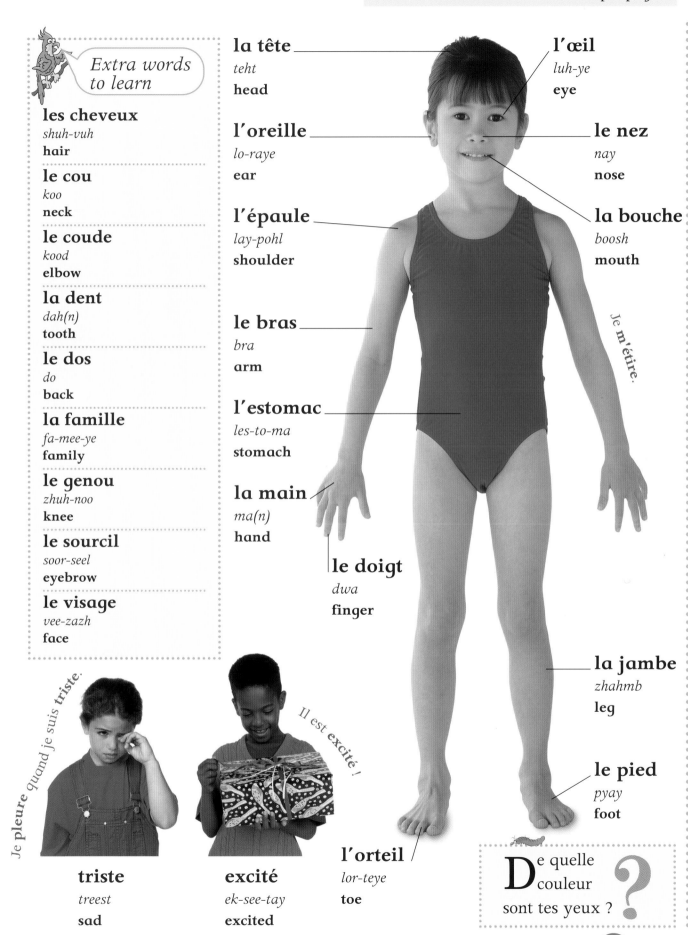

Extra words to learn

les cheveux
shuh-vuh
hair

le cou
koo
neck

le coude
kood
elbow

la dent
dah(n)
tooth

le dos
do
back

la famille
fa-mee-ye
family

le genou
zhuh-noo
knee

le sourcil
soor-seel
eyebrow

le visage
vee-zazh
face

la tête
teht
head

l'oreille
lo-raye
ear

l'épaule
lay-pohl
shoulder

le bras
bra
arm

l'estomac
les-to-ma
stomach

la main
ma(n)
hand

le doigt
dwa
finger

l'œil
luh-ye
eye

le nez
nay
nose

la bouche
boosh
mouth

Je m'étire.

la jambe
zhahmb
leg

le pied
pyay
foot

l'orteil
lor-teye
toe

Je pleure quand je suis triste.

triste
treest
sad

Il est excité !

excité
ek-see-tay
excited

De quelle couleur sont tes yeux ?

All about me

There are about 206 bones in your body!

5

Les vêtements
Clothes

le bouton
button

les chaussettes
shoh-sets
socks

la chemise
shuh-meez
shirt

le jean
jeen
jeans

la fermeture
éclair
zipper

la manche
sleeve

la poche
pocket

le polaire
po-lair
fleece

Mon manteau me tient chaud.

le foulard
foo-lahr
scarf

le gant
glove

les espadrilles
ehs-pa-dree-ye
running shoes

le manteau
mahn-toh
coat

Les vêtements

Les jeans existent depuis plus de 130 ans !

la ceinture
belt

le pantalon
pahn-ta-lo(n)
pants

le tee-shirt
tee-shirt
T-shirt

le short
short
shorts

le maillot de bain
ma-yoh duh ba(n)
bathing suit

le blouson
bloo-zo(n)
jacket

la capuche
hood

la jupe
zhewp
skirt

le jean
jeans

l'imperméable
lam-pair-may-a-bluh
raincoat

Les jeans et les espadrilles sont mes vêtements préférés.

les bottes
bot
boots

A**imes-tu** porter des espadrilles **?**

Jeans are more than 130 years old!

Clothes

La cuisine
Kitchen

la casserole
saucepan

la poêle
pwal
frying pan

l'assiette
la-syet
plate

le four
oven

la cuisinière
kwee-zeen-yair
stove

la cuillère
kwee-yehr
spoon

la tasse
tahss
mug

le livre
book

la casserole
kass-rol
saucepan

Qu'y a-t-il dans la cuillère ?

La première cuisinière à gaz a été fabriquée en 1826.

Merci de **laver la vaisselle.**

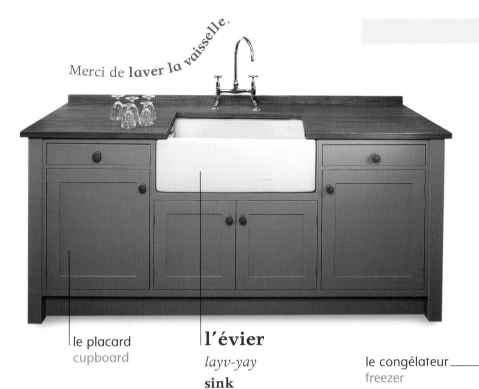

| le placard |
| cupboard |

l'évier
layv-yay
sink

le congélateur
freezer

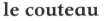

le couteau
koo-toh
knife

la fourchette
foor-shet
fork

le tablier
tab-lee-yay
apron

le gant de cuisine
gah(n) duh kwee-zeen
oven mit

le verre
vair
glass

le réfrigérateur
ray-free-zhair-a-tuhr
fridge

Aimes-tu faire de la pâtisserie ?

Extra words to learn

la bouilloire
booy-wahr
kettle

la cruche
krewsh
jug

le fer à repasser
fair ah ruh-pah-say
iron

le grille-pain
gree-ye-pa(n)
toaster

la machine à laver
ma-sheen ah la-vay
washing machine

le plateau
pla-toh
tray

la poubelle
poo-bell
garbage can

la tasse
tahss
cup

The first gas stove was made in 1826.

Kitchen

La salle de bains

Bathroom

le peigne
pain-ye
comb

la baignoire
bayn-wahr
bath

C'est rigolo de faire des bulles.

le jouet
zhoo-way
toy

l'eau
loh
water

Je mets du dentifrice sur ma **brosse à dents**.

l'éponge
lay-ponzh
sponge

les serviettes
sair-vee-et
towels

le tube
tube

le dentifrice
dahn-tee-freess
toothpaste

la brosse à dents
bros ah dah(n)
toothbrush

Combien d'objets jaunes y a-t-il sur cette page ?

La salle de bains la plus chère a des toilettes en or !

le shampooing
shahm-pwa(n)
shampoo

le miroir
meer-wahr
mirror

la brosse à cheveux
bros ah shuh-vuh
hairbrush

la buée
bway
steam

le maquillage
ma-kee-yazh
make-up

les papiers-mouchoirs
pap-yay moosh-wahr
tissues

se laver
suh la-vay
to wash yourself

la serviette de toilette
sair-vee-et duh twa-let
hand towel

la douche
doosh
shower

le papier de toilette
pap-yay duh twa-let
toilet paper

le savon
sa-vo(n)
soap

les toilettes
twa-let
toilet

le robinet
ro-bee-nay
tap

la serviette
de toilette
hand towel

le savon
soap

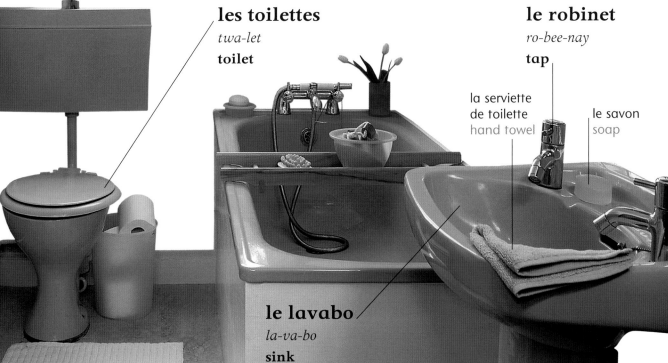

le lavabo
la-va-bo
sink

Bathroom

The most expensive bathroom has a gold toilet!

le réveil
ray-vaye
alarm clock

le lit
lee
bed

l'oreiller
lo-ray-yay
pillow

la couette
koo-et
duvet

la chaise
shehz
chair

12

Ma chambre
My bedroom

la commode
kom-mod
chest of drawers

Je dors dans mon lit.

le jeu électronique
zhuh ay-lek-tro-neek
computer game

Nous jouons à un jeu de plateau.

les échecs
chess

la moquette
moh-ket
carpet

Mon chat dort sous mon lit.

Qu'y a-t-il dans l'armoire ?

les livres
leev-ruh
books

le tapis
ta-pee
rug

La **moquette** est bleue.

Je sais jouer de la **guitare**.

l'armoire
larm-wahr
wardrobe

la guitare
ghee-tar
guitar

le cintre
san-truh
coat hanger

la lampe
lahmp
lamp

le miroir
meer-wahr
mirror

Le jardin
Garden

Extra words to learn

l'arrosoir
lar-rohz-wahr
watering can

le bulbe
bewlb
bulb

la clôture
kloh-tew-ruh
fence

le déplantoir
day-plahnt-wahr
trowel

la feuille
fuh-ye
leaf

le jardinier
zhar-deen-yay
gardener

la pelouse
puh-looz
lawn

la serre
sair
greenhouse

la brouette
broo-et
wheelbarrow

l'arbre
lar-bruh
tree

le tronc
trunk

le râteau
rah-toh
rake

le banc
bench

l'herbe
lairb
grass

la tondeuse à gazon
ton-duhz ah gah-zo(n)
lawn mower

D'habitude, les papillons volent le jour et les papillons de nuit volent la nuit.

De quelle couleur est la coccinelle sur cette page ?

le papillon
pa-pee-yo(n)
butterfly

l'aile
wing

l'escargot
les-kar-goh
snail

le ver
vair
worm

l'abeille
la-baye
bee

la graine
grehn
seed

la coccinelle
kok-see-nel
ladybug

Les **fleurs poussent** dans le **jardin**.

Marie **creuse** dans le **jardin**.

la fleur
fluhr
flower

la chenille
shuh-nee-ye
caterpillar

la terre
tair
soil

la pelle
pel
spade

Usually butterflies fly in the day and moths fly at night.

Garden

La vie en ville
City life

l'autobus
lohto-bews
bus

la maison
may-zo(n)
house

> **Q**uelle heure est-il sur l'horloge bleue **?**

le gratte-ciel
grat-syel
skyscraper

Les villes ont de hauts bâtiments appelés gratte-ciel.

l'horloge
lor-lozh
clock

les appartements
ap-par-tuh-mah(n)
apartments

la rue
rew
street

le magasin
ma-ga-za(n)
store

La vie en ville

Tokyo, au Japon, est la plus grande ville du monde.

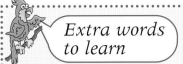

Extra words to learn

l'arrêt d'autobus
lar-reh dohto-bews
bus stop

l'autoroute
loh-toh-root
highway

la banque
bahnk
bank

le café
ka-fay
café

la gare
gar
station

la route
root
road

le trottoir
trot-wahr
sidewalk

l'usine
lew-zeen
factory

le téléphone
tay-lay-fon
phone

le panneau
pan-noh
sign

les feux de signalisation
fuh duh seen-ya-lee-za-syo(n)
traffic lights

le réverbère
ray-vair-bair
street light

le cinéma
see-nay-ma
movie theatre

le carrefour
kar-foor
crossing

le taxi
tak-see
taxi

l'hôtel
lo-tel
hotel

Tokyo, in Japan, is the biggest city in the world.

City life

le cerf-volant
sair-vo-lah(n)
kite

la corde à sauter
kord ah soh-tay
skipping rope

**la planche
à roulettes**
plahnsh a roo-leht
skateboard

les fleurs
fluhr
flowers

le tourniquet
toor-nee-kay
roundabout

Au parc
In the park

J'adore sauter à la corde !

As-tu un cerf-volant ?

la fille
fee-ye
girl

Trois **enfants** jouent sur le **tourniquet**.

18

Les **oiseaux** chantent.

l'arbre
lar-bruh
tree

la balançoire
ba-lahn-swahr
swing

le garçon
gar-so(n)
boy

le ballon de soccer
ba-lo(n) duh sok-uhr
soccer ball

Mon **jeu préféré** est le soccer.

le papillon
pa-pee-yo(n)
butterfly

l'oiseau
lwa-zoh
bird

le vélo
vay-lo
bike

la feuille
fuh-ye
leaf

l'herbe
lairb
grass

19

Les loisirs

Hobbies

*Mes **fleurs** poussent.*

*Je suis **prête** à **aller** nager.*

faire du camping

fair dew kahm-peeng

camping

la natation

na-ta-syo(n)

swimming

le jardinage

zhar-dee-nazh

gardening

observer les oiseaux

ob-zair-vay layz wa-zoh

bird-watching

jouer d'un instrument

zhoo-ay dan an-strew-mah(n)

playing an instrument

*Mathilde **s'entraîne** tous les jours.*

faire de la danse

fair duh la dahnss

dancing

Le surf a commencé à Hawaï, aux Etats-Unis, il y a environ 300 ans.

Les loisirs

Quel est ton
Qloisir préféré ?

Extra words to learn

le chant
shah(n)
singing

collectionner
kol-lek-syo-nay
collecting

le dessin
de-sa(n)
drawing

faire du patin en ligne
fair dew pa-ta(n) ah(n) leen-ye
rollerblading

faire du théâtre
fair dew tay-a-truh
acting

faire du vélo
fair dew vay-lo
cycling

faire la cuisine
fair la kwee-zeen
cooking

la lecture
lek-tewr
reading

le surf
surf
surfing

Je **saute** et je **m'étire** à la gymnastique.

la gymnastique
zheem-nas-teek
gymnastics

prendre une photo
prahn-druh ewn fo-toh
taking a photo

la peinture
pan-tewr
painting

l'écriture
lay-kree-tewr
writing

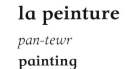

Surfing began in Hawaii, USA, about 300 years ago.

Hobbies

La nourriture

Food

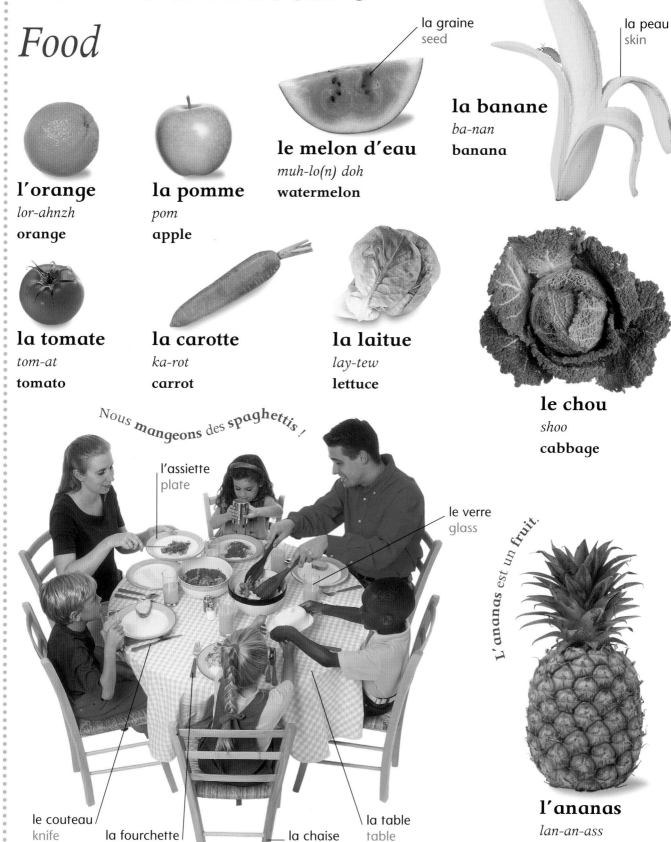

l'orange
lor-ahnzh
orange

la pomme
pom
apple

la graine
seed

le melon d'eau
muh-lo(n) doh
watermelon

la peau
skin

la banane
ba-nan
banana

la tomate
tom-at
tomato

la carotte
ka-rot
carrot

la laitue
lay-tew
lettuce

le chou
shoo
cabbage

*Nous **mangeons** des **spaghettis** !*

l'assiette
plate

le verre
glass

*L'ananas est un **fruit**.*

le couteau
knife

la fourchette
fork

la chaise
chair

la table
table

l'ananas
lan-an-ass
pineapple

22 La carotte est un légume et une racine !

la pomme de terre
pom duh tair
potato

l'œuf
luhf
egg

le yogourt
yoh-goor
yogurt

le lait
lay
milk

la confiture
kon-fee-tewr
jam

Q ue manges-tu au petit-déjeuner ?

 J'aime le **pain** avec du **miel**.

le pain
pa(n)
bread

le beurre
buhr
butter

le miel
myel
honey

les pâtes
paht
pasta

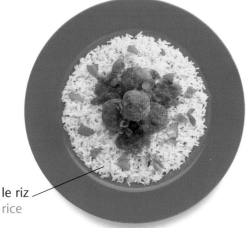

le riz
rice

la viande
vyanhnd
meat

Extra words to learn

le biscuit
bee-skwee
cookie

la farine
far-een
flour

le fruit
frwee
fruit

le légume
lay-gewm
vegetable

l'oignon
lohn-yo(n)
onion

le poulet
poo-lay
chicken

la salade
sal-ad
salad

les spaghettis
spa-get-ee
spaghetti

le sucre
soo-kruh
sugar

Food

A carrot is a vegetable and a root!

Les courses
Shopping

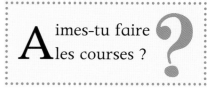

A imes-tu faire les courses ?

le marché
mar-shay
market

le prix
price

l'argent
lar-zhahn
money

le sac
sak
shopping bag

Je dois acheter des œufs.

Nous attendons dans la queue.

le chariot d'épicerie
shar-yoh day-pee-suh-ree
shopping cart

le panier
pan-yay
basket

Le premier chariot d'épicerie a été inventé il y a plus de 60 ans !

la serveuse
sair-vuhz
waitress

le café
ka-fay
café

la liste de provisions
leest duh proh-vee-zyo(n)
shopping list

le supermarché
soo-pair-mar-shay
supermarket

la boulangerie
boo-lahn-zhree
bakery

la librairie
leeb-rair-ee
bookstore

Elle a beaucoup de **sacs** *!*

l'acheteuse
lash-tuhz
shopper

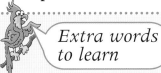

Extra words to learn

l'addition
lad-dee-syo(n)
bill

la caisse
kehss
checkout

en espèces
ah(n) es-pehss
(in) cash

faire les courses
fair lay koorss
to go shopping

le magasin
ma-ga-za(n)
store

le prix
pree
price

le ticket de caisse
tee-kay duh kehss
receipt

le vendeur
vahn-duhr
sales person

Shopping

The first shopping cart was invented more than 60 years ago!

la boisson
bwa-so(n)
drink

les sandwichs
sahnd-weetsh
sandwiches

**les cartes
d'anniversaire**
kart dan-ee-vair-sair
birthday cards

les bougies
boo-zhee
candles

**le gâteau
d'anniversaire**
gah-toh dan-ee-vair-sair
birthday cake

À la fête
At the party

C'est rigolo de **jouer** *avec les* **ballons**.

Nous aimons **danser**.

le lecteur de CD
lek-tuhr duh say-day
CD player

le magicien
ma-zhee-sya(n)
magician

Vois-tu le **gâteau d'anniversaire** ?

les décorations
day-ko-ra-syo(n)
decorations

Bon anniversaire !

C'est incroyable !

Je veux ouvrir les cadeaux.

les cadeaux
ka-doh
gifts

Vois-tu les cartes d'anniversaire ?

les ballons
bal-o(n)
balloons

l'appareil photo
lap-pa-ray fo-toh
camera

les biscuits
bee-skwee
cookies

la crème glacée
krehm glasay
ice cream

les bonbons
bo(n)-bo(n)
candies

Temps libre
Free time

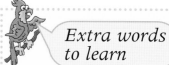

le jeu de plateau
zhuh duh pla-toh
board game

le ballon
bal-o(n)
ball

le robot
ro-boh
robot

les dés
day
dice

l'ordinateur portable
lor-dee-na-tuhr por-ta-bluh
laptop

les blocs
blok
toy blocks

cache-cache
kash-kash
hide-and-seek

le jeu
zhuh
game

le jouet
zhoo-way
toy

la marionnette
mar-yon-net
puppet

le masque
mask
mask

la poupée
poo-pay
doll

le théâtre
thay-a-truh
theatre

le crayon
de couleur
coloured pencil

le dessin
de-sa(n)
drawing

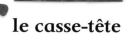

le casse-tête
kahs-teht
puzzle

le train
tra(n)
train

Le premier ordinateur portable a été fabriqué il y a plus de 20 ans.

les cartes
kart
cards

les CD
say-day
CDs

le lecteur de CD
lek-tuhr duh say-day
CD player

le jeu électronique
zhuh ay-lek-tro-neek
computer game

Nous adorons les **spectacles de marionnettes**.

le casque
helmet

Il bouge très vite !

la marionnette
puppet

faire du patin en ligne
fair dew pa-ta(n) ah(n) leen-ye
rollerblading

le spectacle de marionnettes
spek-tak-luh duh mar-yon-net
puppet show

l'ours
en peluche
teddy bear

le déguisement
day-gheez-mah(n)
costume

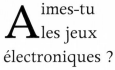

Aimes-tu
les jeux
électroniques ?

Free time

Les moyens de transport

Transport

l'avion
lav-yo(n)
plane

le traversier
tra-vehr-syay
ferry

le bateau à voiles
ba-toh ah vwal
sailboat

le taxi
tak-see
taxi

Les **gens** voyagent en **autobus**.

le camion
kam-yo(n)
truck

le vélo
vay-lo
bike

l'autobus
lohto-bews
bus

Pour les secours

To the rescue

l'échelle
ladder

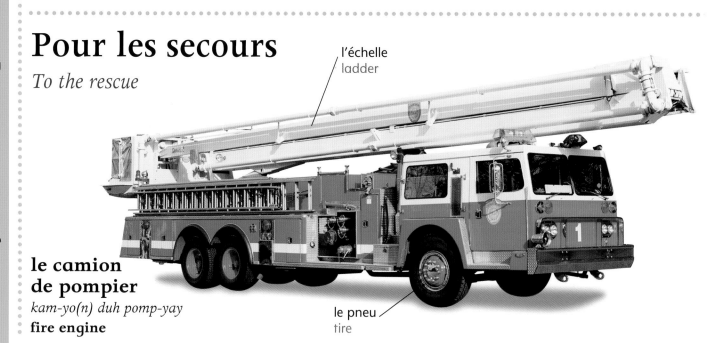

le camion
de pompier
kam-yo(n) duh pomp-yay
fire engine

le pneu
tire

Le camion de pompier le plus rapide a atteint 655 kilomètres-heure en 1998 !

Une montgolfière vole dans le ciel.

le panier
basket

la montgolfière
mohn-golf-yair
hot-air balloon

le train
tra(n)
train

les bagages
luggage

la voiture
vwah-tewr
car

la moto
moh-toh
motorcycle

la roue
wheel

l'hélicoptère de police
lay-lee-kop-tair duh po-leess
police helicopter

la voiture de police
vwa-tewr duh po-leess
police car

Combien de roues y a-t-il sur cette page ?

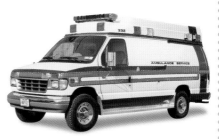

l'ambulance
lahm-bew-lahnss
ambulance

The fastest fire engine reached 655 kilometres per hour in 1998!

Les animaux de la jungle

Jungle animals

l'oiseau-mouche
lwa-zoh-moosh
hummingbird

la chauve-souris
shohv soo-ree
bat

l'aile
wing

le chimpanzé
shahm-pahn-zay
chimpanzee

la fourmi
foor-mee
ant

le papillon
pa-pee-yo(n)
butterfly

l'araignée
lar-ehn-yay
spider

le gorille
go-ree-ye
gorilla

le papillon de nuit
pa-pee-yo(n) duh nwee
moth

Quels animaux peuvent voler sur cette page **?**

le crocodile
kro-ko-deel
crocodile

le perroquet
pair-o-kay
parrot

Le toucan prend la **nourriture** avec son **bec**.

l'œil
eye

le bec
beak

le toucan
too-kah(n)
toucan

la griffe
claw

Extra words to learn

l'aigle
lay-gluh
eagle

l'arbre
lar-bruh
tree

la forêt tropicale
for-eh tro-pee-kal
rainforest

l'insecte
lan-sekt
insect

le lézard
lay-zar
lizard

le mammifère
ma-mee-fair
mammal

l'oiseau
lwa-zoh
bird

le scarabée
ska-ra-bay
beetle

le serpent
sair-pah(n)
snake

la grenouille
gruh-noo-ye
frog

la patte
foot

les rayures
stripes

les taches
spots

le tigre
tee-gruh
tiger

le léopard
lay-o-par
leopard

Jungle animals

The biggest jungle in the world is in South America.

33

Les animaux du monde *World animals*

le koala
ko-a-la
koala

le chevreuil
shuh-vruh-ye
deer

le panda
pahn-da
panda

La girafe a un long cou !

la patte
paw

le lion
lee-yo(n)
lion

la girafe
zhee-raf
giraffe

l'ours blanc
loorss blah(n)
polar bear

le bec
beak

la queue
tail

le manchot
mahn-shoh
penguin

Extra words to learn

l'alligator
lal-ee-gah-tor
alligator

le babouin
ba-bwa(n)
baboon

la chauve-souris
shohv soo-ree
bat

le faucon
foh-ko(n)
hawk

le loup
loo
wolf

le pélican
pay-lee-kah(n)
pelican

le renard
ruh-nar
fox

la tortue de mer
tor-tew duh mair
turtle

Combien d'oiseaux y a-t-il sur cette page ?

La girafe a le même nombre d'os que toi dans le cou !

L'éléphant prend la nourriture avec sa trompe.

le chameau
sha-moh
camel

les rayures
stripes

le zèbre
zeh-bruh
zebra

la trompe
trunk

l'éléphant
lay-lay-fah(n)
elephant

le kangourou
kahn-goo-roo
kangaroo

la queue
tail

l'ours
loorss
bear

la griffe
claw

le dauphin
doh-fa(n)
dolphin

la palme
flipper

le rhinocéros
ree-no-say-ros
rhinoceros

A giraffe has the same number of bones in its neck as you!

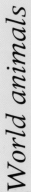

World animals

35

À la ferme
On the farm

le champ
shah(m)
field

le tracteur
trak-tuhr
tractor

le blé
blay
wheat

les agneaux
an-yoh
lambs

le chien de berger
shya(n) duh bair-zhay
sheepdog

La **fermière** utilise le **tracteur**.

la fermière
fairm-yair
farmer

La **vache** mange l'**herbe** dans le **champ**.

Anne donne du **lait** à l'**agneau**.

36

la moissonneuse-batteuse
mwa-son-nuhz bat-tuhz
combine harvester

la clôture
kloh-tew-ruh
fence

Le cheval est brun et blanc.

le canard
ka-nar
duck

Le poussin est près de sa mère.

la vache
vash
cow

le foin
fwa(n)
hay

le cheval
shuh-val
horse

le poulet
poo-lay
chicken

les canetons
ka-nuh-to(n)
ducklings

L'océan

Ocean

le bateau de pêche

ba-toh duh pehsh

fishing boat

la mouette

moo-wet

seagull

La voile est jaune et violette.

la voile
sail

le bateau à voiles

ba-toh ah vwal

sailboat

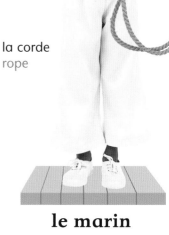

la corde
rope

le marin

mar-a(n)

sailor

Extra words to learn

l'ancre

lahn-kruh

anchor

la bouée

boo-way

buoy

le canot

kanoh

row boat

la mer

mair

sea

la pêche

pehsh

fishing

le port

por

harbour

la vague

vag

wave

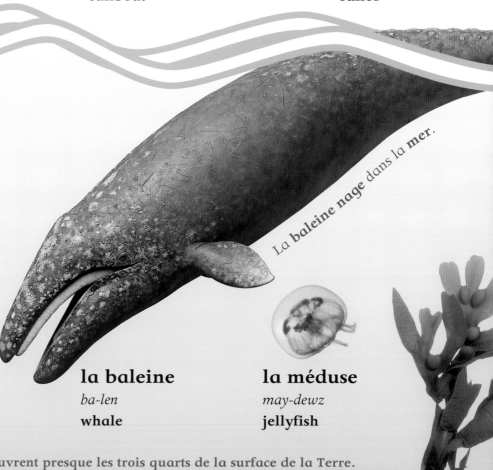

La baleine nage dans la mer.

la baleine

ba-len

whale

la méduse

may-dewz

jellyfish

L'océan

Les océans couvrent presque les trois quarts de la surface de la Terre.

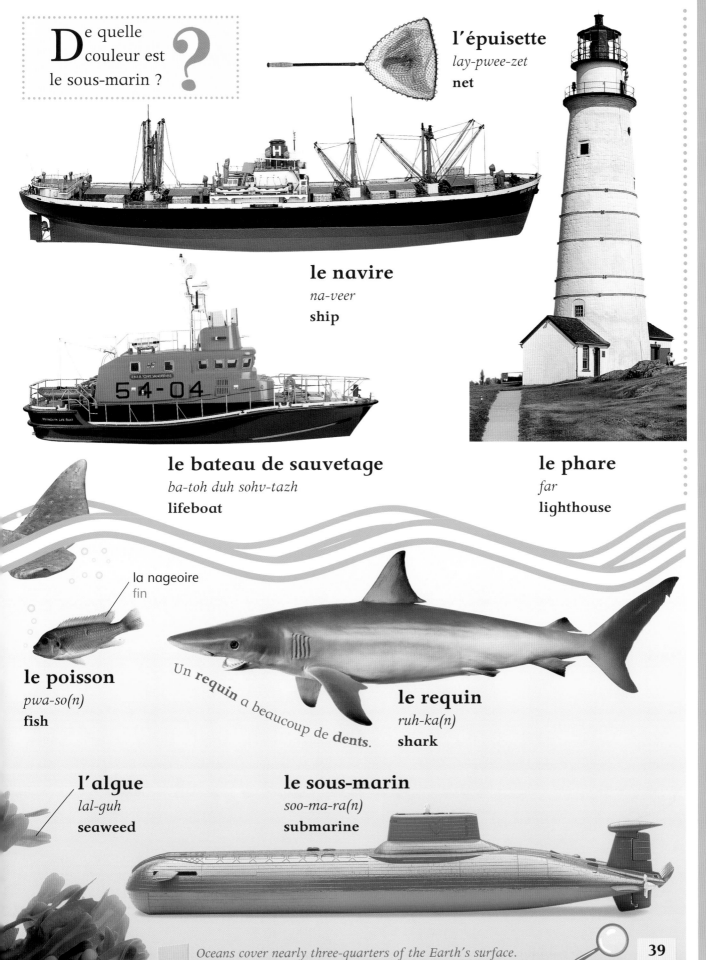

De quelle couleur est le sous-marin ?

l'épuisette
lay-pwee-zet
net

le navire
na-veer
ship

le bateau de sauvetage
ba-toh duh sohv-tazh
lifeboat

le phare
far
lighthouse

la nageoire
fin

le poisson
pwa-so(n)
fish

Un **requin** a beaucoup de **dents**.

le requin
ruh-ka(n)
shark

l'algue
lal-guh
seaweed

le sous-marin
soo-ma-ra(n)
submarine

Ocean

Oceans cover nearly three-quarters of the Earth's surface.

La nature

Nature

Le **nénuphar pousse** dans l'eau.

le bec
beak

le canard
ka-nar
duck

la plante
plahnt
plant

la libellule
lee-bel-lewl
dragonfly

le nénuphar
nay-new-far
water lily

Beaucoup d'**animaux vivent** près des **étangs**.

le cygne
seen-ye
swan

le crapaud
kra-poo
toad

40 D'habitude, les crapauds ont la peau rugueuse et les grenouilles ont la peau lisse !

Les têtards nagent dans les étangs.

le nid
nee
nest

les têtards
the-tar
tadpoles

l'antenne
antenna

la guêpe
gehp
wasp

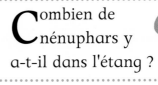

l'aile
wing

la mouche
moosh
fly

Combien de nénuphars y a-t-il dans l'étang ?

l'étang
lay-tah(n)
pond

le hibou
ee-boo
owl

la grenouille
gruh-noo-ye
frog

Extra words to learn

l'eau
loh
water

l'habitat
la-bee-ta
habitat

le héron
air-o(n)
heron

l'insecte
lan-sekt
insect

le lapin
lap-a(n)
rabbit

la mauvaise herbe
moh-vayz airb
weed

l'oiseau
lwa-zoh
bird

le papillon
pa-pee-yo(n)
butterfly

Toads usually have rough skin and frogs have smooth skin!

Nature

le seau
soh
bucket

la pelle
pel
spade

le crabe
krab
crab

le coquillage
ko-kee-yazh
shell

les galets
ga-lay
pebbles

À la plage
At the beach

J'adore **nager** dans la **mer** !

Aimes-tu **aller** à la **plage** ?

Je **joue** sous mon **parasol**.

le parasol
umbrella

le rocher
ro-shay
rock

la crème solaire
suntan lotion

les mouettes
moo-wet
seagulls

Nous adorons **jouer** avec le **sable**.

Je porte des **lunettes de natation**.

le maillot de bain
bathing suit

l'étoile de mer
lay-twal duh mair
starfish

la crème glacée
krehm glasay
ice cream

l'algue
lal-guh
seaweed

Nous **construisons** un **château de sable**.

les lunettes de natation
lew-net duh na-ta-syo(n)
swim goggles

la chaise longue
shayz long-uh
deck chair

le chapeau de soleil
sha-poh duh so-laye
sunhat

le sable
sah-bluh
sand

le château de sable
sha-toh duh sah-bluh
sandcastle

L'école
School

les ciseaux
see-zoh
scissors

les crayons de couleur
kra-yo(n) duh koo-luhr
coloured pencils

le tableau noir
tab-loh nwahr
blackboard

la règle
reh-gluh
ruler

la gomme
gom
eraser

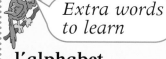

Extra words to learn

l'alphabet
lal-fa-bay
alphabet

la chaise
shehz
chair

le dessin
de-sa(n)
drawing

l'écriture
lay-kree-tewr
writing

la lecture
lek-tewr
reading

le maître
meh-truh
teacher

la salle de classe
sal duh klahss
classroom

les sciences
see-yahnss
science

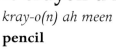

le crayon à mine
kray-o(n) ah meen
pencil

le stylo
stee-loh
pen

le carnet
notebook

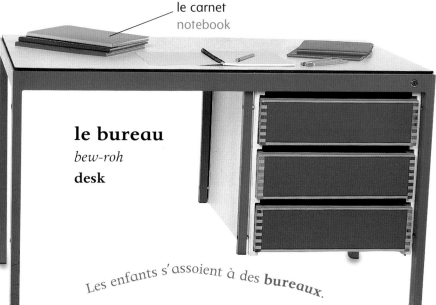

le bureau
bew-roh
desk

Les enfants s'assoient à des **bureaux**.

L'école

Le crayon à mine le plus long du monde fait presque 20 mètres de long.

Vois-tu la **pomme** dans la **boîte-repas** ?

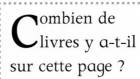

Combien de livres y a-t-il sur cette page ?

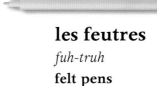

les feutres
fuh-truh
felt pens

la boîte-repas
bwat ruh-pah
lunch box

Trouve ton **pays** sur le **globe**.

le cahier
ka-yay
exercise book

le globe
glob
globe

le cartable
school bag

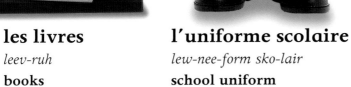

les livres
leev-ruh
books

l'uniforme scolaire
lew-nee-form sko-lair
school uniform

l'ordinateur
lor-dee-na-tuhr
computer

The longest pencil in the world is almost 20 metres long.

Les sports
Sports

Je porte un **casque**.

le casque
helmet

la roue
wheel

faire du vélo
fair dew vay-lo
cycling

le ski
skee
skiing

la raquette
rak-et
racket

**le patinage
sur glace**
*pa-tee-nazh
soor glass*
ice skating

la gymnastique
zheem-nas-teek
gymnastics

Nous jouons au basketball.

Delphine **veut marquer** un **but**.

le tee-shirt
T-shirt

le short
shorts

le basketball
basket-bohl
basketball

le golf
golf
golf

le soccer
sok-uhr
soccer

Il y a environ 28 sports aux Jeux olympiques d'été.

Extra words to learn

l'athlétisme
lat-lay-tee-smah
athletics

le baseball
bayz-bohl
baseball

l'exercice
lek-sair-seess
exercise

le hockey
ok-ay
hockey

le hockey sur gazon
ok-ay soor gah-zo(n)
field hockey

le judo
zhew-do
judo

le karaté
ka-ra-tay
karate

la natation
na-ta-syo(n)
swimming

Aimes-tu faire du sport ?

la voile
sail

le gilet de sauvetage
life jacket

la plongée
plon-zhay
diving

faire de la voile
fair duh la vwal
sailing

Je **tire** sur les **rames**.

la balle
ball

le gant
glove

la rame
oar

faire de l'aviron
fair duh lav-ee-ro(n)
rowing

le bâton
bah-to(n)
bat

le cheval
horse

la raquette
racket

le rugby
rewg-bee
rugby

la course à pied
koorss ah pyay
running

l'équitation
lay-keet-a-syo(n)
horseback riding

le tennis
ten-neess
tennis

Sports

Les animaux familiers

Pets

Mon **chien** s'appelle Toby.

la nourriture
food

le chiot
shyoh
puppy

Une **tortue bouge** très **lentement**.

le hamster
am-stair
hamster

la tortue
tor-tew
tortoise

le lapin
lap-(a)n
rabbit

le cochon d'Inde
ko-sho(n) dand
guinea pig

le collier
collar

De quelles couleurs sont les poils du cochon d'Inde ?

le chat
sha
cat

le poisson rouge
pwa-so(n) roozh
goldfish

Les animaux familiers

Un chat dort environ 16 heures par jour.

les poils
fur

le chaton

sha-to(n)

kitten

la langue
tongue

le chien

shya(n)

dog

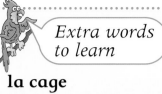
Extra words to learn

la cage
kahzh
cage

le collier
kol-yay
collar

la griffe
greef
claw

la nageoire
nazh-wahr
fin

le panier
pan-yay
basket

la patte
pat
paw

la plume
plewm
feather

le/la vétérinaire
vay-tayr-ee-nair
vet

Un **perroquet** a des **plumes** de toutes les **couleurs**.

le bec
beak

le perroquet

pair-o-kay

parrot

l'oiseau

lwa-zoh

bird

Paul brosse le **cheval**.

les moustaches
whiskers

la queue
tail

la souris

soo-ree

mouse

le cheval

shuh-val

horse

A cat sleeps about 16 hours a day.

Les couleurs et les formes

Colours and shapes

rouge
roozh
red

orange
or-ahnzh
orange

jaune
zhohn
yellow

vert
vair
green

bleu
bluh
blue

violet
vyo-lay
purple

rose
rohz
pink

brun
bra(n)
brown

noir
nwahr
black

courbe
curved

droit
straight

Q uelle est
ta couleur
préférée ?

50

Toutes les couleurs sont un mélange de rouge, de jaune et de bleu !

l'arc-en-ciel
rainbow

le carré
kar-ray
square

le cercle
sair-kluh
circle

le triangle
tree-yahn-gluh
triangle

le losange
lo-zahnzh
diamond

l'étoile
lay-twal
star

le rectangle
rek-tahn-gluh
rectangle

 *Extra words to learn*

blanc
blah(n)
white

le cœur
kuhr
heart

coloré
ko-lo-ray
colourful

courbe
koorb
curved

le demi-cercle
duh-mee sair-kluh
semicircle

droit
drwa
straight

l'ovale
lo-val
oval

rond
ro(n)
round

le cube
kewb
cube

le ballon
bal-o(n)
ball

Colours and shapes

All colours are a mixture of red, yellow or blue!

51

Les contraires
Opposites

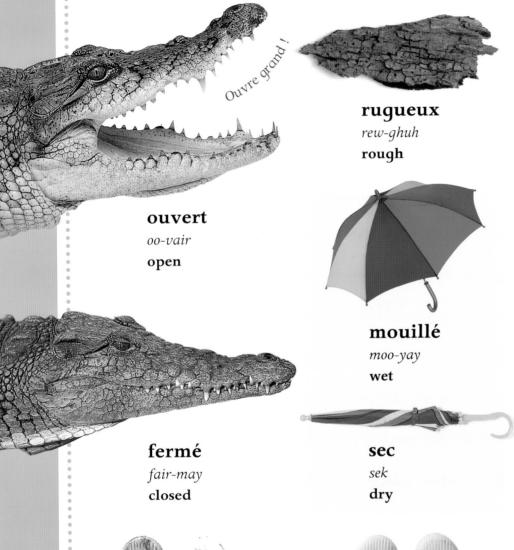

Ouvre grand !

ouvert
oo-vair
open

fermé
fair-may
closed

rugueux
rew-ghuh
rough

lisse
leess
smooth

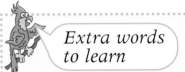

mouillé
moo-yay
wet

sec
sek
dry

sale
sal
dirty

propre
prop-ruh
clean

Extra words to learn

léger
lay-zhay
light

lent
lah(n)
slow

lourd
loor
heavy

nouveau
noo-voh
new

plein
pla(n)
full

rapide
rap-eed
fast

vide
veed
empty

vieux
vyuh
old

La plupart des citrouilles sont orange mais certaines sont blanches ou bleues !

Les contraires

Préfères-tu
les boissons
chaudes ou froides ?

Une **citrouille** devient **grosse** en **automne**.

froid
frwa
cold

chaud
shoh
hot

Ce **légume** est très **fin**.

gros
groh
fat

fin
fa(n)
thin

mou
moo
soft

dur
dewr
hard

Le tournesol a une **grande** tige.

Cette fleur a une **tige courte**.

court
koor
short

grand
grah(n)
tall

petit
puh-tee
small

grand
grah(n)
big

Most pumpkins are orange, but you can grow white and blue ones!

Opposites

le bonhomme de neige
bon-om duh nehzh
snowman

la neige
nehzh
snow

la tuque
tew-kuh
tuque

C'est très venteux.

le parapluie
pa-ra-plwee
umbrella

Le temps qu'il fait
Weather

l'automne
loh-ton
autumn

l'hiver
lee-vair
winter

les flocons de neige
flo-ko(n) duh nehzh
snowflakes

J'ai fait un bonhomme de neige.

Je porte une tuque, un foulard et des gants.

le printemps
pran-tah(m)
spring

J'ai un **parapluie** jaune.

l'été
lay-tay
summer

le soleil
so-laye
sun

Il fait **chaud** au **soleil**.

la pluie
plwee
rain

le nuage
new-azh
cloud

l'arc-en-ciel
lark-ah(n)-syel
rainbow

les lunettes de soleil
lew-net duh so-laye
sunglasses

la casquette
kas-ket
cap

English A–Z

In this section English words are in alphabetical order, followed by the French translation. There is information after each English word to show you what type of word it is. This will help you to make sentences. In French, nouns (naming words) are either masculine or feminine. If the French word has *un* or *le* before it, it is masculine (m), if it has *une* or *la*, it is feminine (f).

(n) = noun (a naming word). Either masculine or feminine. Feminine nouns usually have an "e" at the end.

(adj) = adjective (a describing word). These words can change depending whether the noun they are describing is masculine (m) or feminine (f).

(adv) = adverb (a word that gives more information about a verb, an adjective, or another adverb)

(conj) = conjunction (a joining word, e.g., and)

(prep) = preposition (e.g., about)

(pron) = pronoun (e.g., he, she, it)

(article) = (e.g., a, an, the)

apple
la pomme

a (article)
un/une
a(n)/ewn

about (adv)
environ
ahn-veer-o(n)

about (prep)
sur
soor

above (prep)
au-dessus de
oh duhs-ew duh

accident (n)
un accident
ak-see-dah(n)

across (prep)
de l'autre côté de
duh loh-truh koh-tay duh

activity (n)
une activité
ak-tee-vee-tay

address (n)
une adresse
a-dress

adult (n)
un/une adulte
ad-ewlt

adventure (n)
une aventure
av-ahn-tewr

after (prep)
après
ap-reh

afternoon (n)
un après-midi
ap-reh mee-dee

again (adv)
encore
ahn-kor

age (n)
l'âge (m)
lahzh

air (n)
l'air (m)
lair

airplane (n)
un avion
av-yo(n)

airport (n)
un aéroport
a-ay-ro-por

alarm clock (n)
un réveil
ray-vaye

all (adj)
tout (m) toute (f)
too/toot

alligator (n)
un alligator
al-ee-gah-tor

almost (adv)
presque
presk

alone (adj)
seul (m) seule (f)
suhl

alphabet (n)
l'alphabet (m)
lal-fa-bay

already (adv)
déjà
day-zha

also (adv)
aussi
oh-see

always (adv)
toujours
too-zhoor

amazing (adj)
incroyable
an-krwa-ya-bluh

ambulance (n)
une ambulance
ahm-bew-lahnss

an (article)
un/une
a(n)/ewn

anchor (n)
une ancre
ahn-kruh

and (conj)
et
eh

angry (adj)
en colère
ah(n) ko-lehr

animal (n)
un animal
an-ee-mal

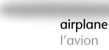

airplane
l'avion

A
B
C
D
E
F
G
H
I
J
K
L
M
N
O
P
Q
R
S
T
U
V
W
X
Y
Z

ankle (n)
une **cheville**
shuh-vee-ye

answer (n)
une **réponse**
ray-ponss

ant (n)
une **fourmi**
foor-mee

antenna (n)
une **antenne**
ahn-ten

anybody (pron)
n'importe **qui**
nam-port kee

anything (pron)
n'importe **quoi**
nam-port kwa

apart (adv)
séparément
say-pa-ray-mah(n)

apartment (n)
un **appartement**
ap-par-tuh-mah(n)

appearance (n)
une **apparence**
ap-par-ahnss

apple (n)
une **pomme**
pom

armchair
le fauteuil

apron (n)
un **tablier**
tab-lee-yay

arch (n)
une **arche**
arsh

area (n)
une **région**
ray-zhyo(n)

arm (n)
un **bras**
bra

armchair (n)
un **fauteuil**
foh-tuh-ye

army (n)
une **armée**
ar-may

around (prep)
autour
oh-toor

arrival (n)
une **arrivée**
ar-ree-vay

arrow (n)
une **flèche**
flehsh

art (n)
l'art **(m)**
lar

astronaut
l'astronaute

artist (n)
un/une **artiste**
ar-teest

assistant (n)
un **assistant**
a-seess-tah(n)

une **assistante**
a-seess-tahnt

astronaut (n)
un/une **astronaute**
astro-noht

astronomer (n)
un/une **astronome**
astro-nom

athletics (n)
l'athlétisme **(m)**
lat-lay-tee-smah

atlas (n)
un **atlas**
at-lahs

attic (n)
un **grenier**
gruhn-yay

aunt (n)
une **tante**
tahnt

autumn (n)
l'automne **(m)**
loh-ton

avocado (n)
un **avocat**
av-o-ka

away (adj)
absent **(m)**
ap-sah(n)

absente **(f)**
ap-sahnt

avocado
l'avocat

B

balloon
le ballon

baboon (n)
un **babouin**
ba-bwa(n)

baby (n)
un **bébé**
bay-bay

back (body) (n)
un **dos**
do

back (adv)
à l'**arrière**
ah lar-yehr

backpack (n)
un **sac à dos**
sak ah do

backwards (adv)
en **arrière**
ah(n) ar-yehr

bear
l'ours

bad (adj)
mauvais (m)
moh-vay

mauvaise (f)
moh-vayz

badge (n)
un **insigne**
an-seen-ye

badminton (n)
le **badminton**
bad-meen-ton

bag (n)
un **sac**
sak

bakery (n)
une **boulangerie**
boo-lahn-zhree

balcony (n)
un **balcon**
bal-ko(n)

ball (n)
un **ballon**
bal-o(n)

une **balle**
bal

ballet dancer (n)
un **danseur**
de **ballet**
dahn-suhr duh ba-leh

une **danseuse**
de **ballet**
dahn-suhz duh ba-leh

balloon (n)
un **ballon**
bal-o(n)

banana (n)
une **banane**
ba-nan

band (n)
une **bande**
bahnd

bank (money) (n)
une **banque**
bahnk

bank (river) (n)
une **rive**
reev

barbecue (n)
un **barbecue**
bar-buhk-yew

barn (n)
une **grange**
grahnzh

baseball (n)
le **baseball**
bayz-bohl

basket (n)
un **panier**
pan-yay

basketball (n)
le **basketball**
basket-bohl

bat (animal) (n)
une **chauve-souris**
shohv soo-ree

bat (sports) (n)
un **bâton**
bah-to(n)

bath (n)
une **baignoire**
bayn-wahr

bathing suit (n)
un **maillot de bain**
ma-yoh duh ba(n)

bathroom (n)
une **salle de bains**
sal duh ba(n)

battery (n)
une **pile**
peel

battle (n)
une **bataille**
bat-ah-ye

bat
la chauve-souris

beach (n)
une **plage**
plazh

bead (n)
une **perle**
pairl

beak (n)
un **bec**
behk

beans (n)
les **haricots**
ar-ee-koh

bear (n)
un **ours**
oorss

beard (n)
une **barbe**
barb

beautiful (adj)
beau (m) **belle** (f)
boh/bell

beauty (n)
la **beauté**
boh-tay

because (conj)
parce que
par-suh-kuh

bed (n)
un **lit**
lee

bedroom (n)
une **chambre**
shahm-bruh

bee (n)
une **abeille**
a-baye

A B C D E F G H I J K L M N O P Q R S T U V W X Y Z

beetle (n)
un scarabée
ska-ra-bay

before (prep)
avant
av-ah(n)

behind (prep)
derrière
dair-yehr

bell (n)
une cloche
klosh

below (prep)
au-dessous de
oh-duh-soo duh

belt (n)
une ceinture
san-tewr

bench (n)
un banc
bah(n)

best (adj)
mieux
myuh

better (adj)
meilleur (m)
may-yuhr
meilleure (f)

binoculars
les jumelles

bike
le vélo

saddle
la selle

pedal
la pédale

tire
le pneu

wheel
la roue

between (prep)
entre
ahn-truh

big (large) (adj)
gros (m) grosse (f)
groh/grohss

big (tall) (adj)
grand (m)
grah(n)
grande (f)
grahnd

bike (n)
un vélo
vay-lo

bill (n)
une addition
ad-dee-syo(n)

billion
un milliard
meel-yar

binoculars (n)
les jumelles
zhew-mel

bird (n)
un oiseau
wa-zoh

birthday (n)
un anniversaire
an-ee-vair-sair

birthday cake (n)
un gâteau
d'anniversaire
gah-toh dan-ee-vair-sair

birthday card (n)
une carte
d'anniversaire
kart dan-ee-vair-sair

black (adj)
noir (m) noire (f)
nwahr

blackboard (n)
un tableau noir
tab-loh nwahr

blanket (n)
une couverture
koo-vair-tewr

blonde (adj)
blond (m)
bloh(n)

blonde (f)
blohnd

blood (n)
le sang
sah(n)

blouse (n)
un chemisier
shuh-meez-yay

blue (adj)
bleu (m) bleue (f)
bluh

board (notice) (n)
un panneau
pan-noh

board game (n)
un jeu de plateau
zhuh duh pla-toh

boat (n)
un bateau
ba-toh

A B C D E F G H I J K L M N O P Q R S T U V W X Y Z

body (n)
un **corps**
kor

bone (n)
un **os**
oss

book (n)
un **livre**
leev-ruh

bookstore (n)
une **librairie**
leeb-rair-ee

boot (n)
une **botte**
bot

boring (adj)
ennuyeux (m)
ahn-wee-yuh
ennuyeuse (f)
ahn-wee-yuhz

bottle (n)
une **bouteille**
boo-taye

bottom (n)
le **fond**
foh(n)

bowl (cereal) (n)
un **bol**
bol

box (n)
une **boîte**
bwat

boy (n)
un **garçon**
gar-so(n)

boyfriend (n)
un **petit ami**
puh-tee-ta-mee

bracelet (n)
un **bracelet**
bra-slay

brain (n)
un **cerveau**
sair-voh

branch (n)
une **branche**
brahnsh

brave (adj)
courageux (m)
koor-a-zhuh
courageuse (f)
koor-a-zhuhz

bread (n)
un **pain**
pa(n)

break (n)
une **pause**
pohz

breakfast (n)
un **petit-déjeuner**
puh-tee day-zhuh-nay

breeze (n)
une **brise**
breez

bubbles
les bulles

butterfly
le papillon

bridge (n)
un **pont**
po(n)

bright (adj)
brillant (m)
bree-yah(n)
brillante (f)
bree-yahnt

broken (adj)
cassé (m) cassée (f)
kah-say

broom (n)
un **balai**
ba-lay

brother (n)
un **frère**
frair

brown (adj)
brun
bra(n)

bubble (n)
une **bulle**
bewl

bucket (n)
un **seau**
soh

building (n)
un **bâtiment**
bah-tee-mah(n)

bulb (light) (n)
une **ampoule**
ahm-pool

bulb (plant) (n)
un **bulbe**
bewlb

buoy (n)
une **bouée**
boo-way

bus (n)
un **autobus**
ohto-bews

bus stop (n)
un **arrêt d'autobus**
ar-reh dohto-bews

bush (n)
un **buisson**
bwee-so(n)

business (n)
les **affaires**
a-fair

busy (adj)
occupé (m)
occupée (f)
ok-ew-pay

but (conj)
mais
may

butter (n)
le **beurre**
buhr

butterfly (n)
un **papillon**
pa-pee-yo(n)

button (n)
un **bouton**
boo-to(n)

C

cake
le gâteau

cabbage (n)
un **chou**
shoo

café (n)
un **café**
ka-fay

cage (n)
une **cage**
kahzh

cake (n)
un **gâteau**
gah-toh

calculator (n)
une **calculatrice**
kal-kew-la-treess

calendar (n)
un **calendrier**
kal-ahn-dree-yay

calf (n)
un **veau**
voh

calm (adj)
calme
kalm

camel (n)
un **chameau**
sha-moh

camera (n)
un **appareil photo**
ap-pa-ray fo-toh

can (n)
un **bidon**
bee-do(n)

candle (n)
une **bougie**
boo-zhee

candy (n)
un **bonbon**
bo(n)-bo(n)

canoe (n)
un **canoé**
kan-o-ay

cap (n)
une **casquette**
kas-ket

capital (n)
une **capitale**
ka-pee-tal

car (n)
une **voiture**
vwah-tewr

card (n)
une **carte**
kart

cardboard (n)
le **carton**
kar-to(n)

cards (n)
les **cartes**
kart

careful (adj)
prudent (m)
prew-dah(n)

prudente (f)
prew-dahnt

carpet (n)
une **moquette**
moh-ket

carrot (n)
une **carotte**
ka-rot

cart (n)
une **charrette**
sha-ret

cart (shopping) (n)
un **chariot**
d'épicerie
shar-yoh day-pee-suh-ree

cash (n)
en **espèces**
ah(n) es-pehss

cassette (n)
une **cassette**
ka-set

cat (n)
un **chat**
sha

caterpillar (n)
une **chenille**
shuh-nee-ye

cave (n)
une **grotte**
grot

CD (n)
un **CD**
say-day

CD player (n)
un **lecteur de CD**
lek-tuhr duh say-day

ceiling (n)
un **plafond**
pla-fo(n)

cellar (n)
une **cave**
kav

centre (n)
le **centre**
sahn-truh

cereal (n)
une **céréale**
sair-ay-al

certain (adj)
certain (m)
sair-ta(n)

certaine (f)
sair-tehn

chain (n)
une **chaîne**
shehn

chair (n)
une **chaise**
shehz

challenge (n)
un **défi**
day-fee

change (n)
un **changement**
shahnzh-mah(n)

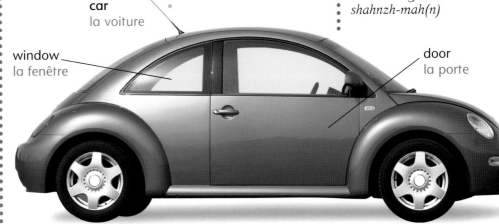

car
la voiture

window
la fenêtre

door
la porte

A
B
C
D
E
F
G
H
I
J
K
L
M
N
O
P
Q
R
S
T
U
V
W
X
Y
Z

cheap (adj)
bon marché
bo(n) mar-shay

checkout (n)
une caisse
kehss

cheese (n)
un fromage
fro-mazh

cheetah (n)
un guépard
gay-par

chef (n)
un/une chef
shef

chess (n)
les échecs
ay-shek

chest (n)
une poitrine
pwa-treen

chest of drawers (n)
une commode
kom-mod

chewing gum (n)
une gomme
à macher
gom a mah-shay

chick (n)
un poussin
poo-sa(n)

chicken (n)
un poulet
poo-lay

child (n)
un/une enfant
ahn-fah(n)

children (n)
les enfants
ahn-fah(n)

chimney (n)
une cheminée
shuh-mee-nay

chimpanzee (n)
un chimpanzé
shahm-pahn-zay

chin (n)
un menton
mahn-to(n)

chocolate (n)
le chocolat
sho-ko-la

Christmas (n)
Noël
no-el

church (n)
une église
ayg-leess

circle (n)
un cercle
sair-kluh

circus (n)
un cirque
seerk

city (n)
une ville
veel

classroom (n)
une salle de classe
sal duh klahss

claw (n)
une griffe
greef

clean (adj)
propre
prop-ruh

clear (adj)
clair (m) claire (f)
klair

clever (adj)
intelligent (m)
an-tel-lee-zhah(n)
intelligente (f)
an-tel-lee-zhahnt

cliff (n)
une falaise
fa-lehz

cloak (n)
une cape
kap

clock (n)
une horloge
or-lozh

close (near) (adj)
proche
prosh

closed (adj)
fermé (m) fermée (f)
fair-may

cloth (n)
un tissu
tee-soo

clothes (n)
les vêtements
veht-mah(n)

cloud (n)
un nuage
new-azh

cloudy (adj)
nuageux (m)
new-azh-uh
nuageuse (f)
new-azh-uhz

clown (n)
un clown
kloon

coach (n)
un autocar
ohto-kar

coast (n)
une côte
koht

coat (n)
un manteau
mahn-toh

coat hanger (n)
un cintre
san-truh

coffee (n)
le café
ka-fay

coin (n)
une pièce
de monnaie
pyehs duh mon-neh

cold (adj)
froid (m)
frwa
froide (f)
frwad

collar (n)
un collier
kol-yay

colour (n)
une couleur
koo-luhr

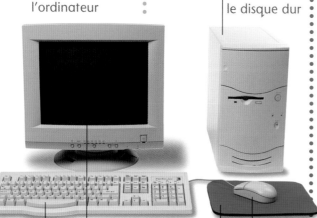

computer
l'ordinateur

hard drive
le disque dur

keyboard
le clavier

screen
l'écran

mouse pad
le tapis de souris

mouse
la souris

compass
la boussole

coloured pencil (n)
un **crayon de couleur**
kra-yo(n) duh koo-luhr

colourful (adj)
coloré (m)
colorée (f)
ko-lo-ray

comb (n)
un **peigne**
pain-ye

combine harvester (n)
une **moissonneuse-batteuse**
mwa-son-nuhz bat-tuhz

comfortable (adj)
confortable
kon-for-ta-bluh

comic (n)
un **comique**
ko-meek

compass (n)
une **boussole**
boo-sol

crab
le crabe

computer (n)
un **ordinateur**
or-dee-na-tuhr

computer game (n)
un **jeu électronique**
zhuh ay-lek-tro-neek

concert (n)
un **concert**
kon-sair

continent (n)
un **continent**
kon-tee-nah(n)

controls (n)
les **commandes**
ko-mahnd

cookie (n)
un **biscuit**
bee-skwee

cool (adj)
frais (m)
fray
fraîche (f)
frehsh

corner (n)
un **coin**
kwa(n)

correct (adj)
juste
zhewst

costume (n)
un **déguisement**
day-gheez-mah(n)

cotton (n)
le **coton**
ko-to(n)

cough (n)
une **toux**
too

country (n)
un **pays**
pay-ee

countryside (n)
la **campagne**
kahm-pan-ye

cousin (n)
un **cousin**
koo-za(n)
une **cousine**
koo-zeen

cow (n)
une **vache**
vash

cowboy (n)
un **cow-boy**
koh-boye

crab (n)
un **crabe**
krab

crane (n)
une **grue**
grew

crayon (n)
un **crayon de couleur**
kray-o(n) duh koo-luhr

cream (n)
la **crème**
krehm

creature (n)
une **bête**
beht

crew (n)
un **équipage**
ay-kee-pazh

crocodile (n)
un **crocodile**
kro-ko-deel

crop (n)
une **récolte**
ray-kolt

crossing (n)
un **carrefour**
kar-foor

crowded (adj)
bondé (m)
bondée (f)
bon-day

crown (n)
une **couronne**
koo-ron

cube (n)
un **cube**
kewb

cup (n)
une **tasse**
tahss

cupboard (n)
un **placard**
pla-kar

curious (adj)
curieux (m)
kew-ree-uh
curieuse (f)
kew-ree-uhz

curly (adj)
frisé (m) frisée (f)
free-zay

curtain (n)
un **rideau**
ree-doh

curved (adj)
courbe
koorb

cushion (n)
un **coussin**
koo-sa(n)

customer (n)
un **client**
klee-ah(n)
une **cliente**
klee-ahnt

crown
la couronne

A
B
C
D
E
F
G
H
I
J
K
L
M
N
O
P
Q
R
S
T
U
V
W
X
Y
Z

D

daisy
la pâquerette

dad (n)
papa
pa-pa

dairy (adj)
laitier (m) laitière (f)
layt-yay/layt-yair

daisy (n)
une pâquerette
pak-uh-ret

dancer (n)
un danseur
dahn-suhr

une danseuse
dahn-suhz

dandelion (n)
un pissenlit
pee-sahn-lee

danger (n)
un danger
dahn-zhay

dangerous (adj)
dangereux (m)
dahn-zhay-ruh

dangereuse (f)
dahn-zhay-ruhz

dark (adj)
sombre
som-bruh

date (n)
une date
dat

daughter (n)
une fille
fee-ye

day (n)
un jour
zhoor

dead (adj)
mort (m) morte (f)
mor/mort

deaf (adj)
sourd (m) sourde (f)
soor/soord

dear (adj)
cher (m) chère (f)
shair

deck (boat) (n)
un pont
po(n)

deck chair (n)
une chaise longue
shayz long-uh

decoration (n)
une décoration
day-ko-ra-syo(n)

deep (adj)
profond (m)
pro-fo(n)

profonde (f)
pro-fond

deer (n)
un chevreuil
shuh-vruh-ye

delicious (adj)
délicieux (m)
day-lee-syuh

délicieuse (f)
day-lee-syuhz

dentist (n)
un/une dentiste
dahn-teest

desert (n)
un désert
day-zair

desk (n)
un bureau
bew-roh

dessert (n)
un dessert
duh-sair

diagram (n)
un diagramme
dya-gram

diamond (shape) (n)
un losange
lo-zahnzh

diary (n)
un journal
zhoor-nal

dice (n)
les dés
day

dictionary (n)
un dictionnaire
deek-syo-nair

different (adj)
différent (m)
dee-fay-rah(n)

différente (f)
dee-fay-rahnt

difficult (adj)
difficile
dee-fee-seel

digital (adj)
digital (m)
digitale (f)
dee-zhee-tal

dining room (n)
une salle à manger
sal ah mahn-zhay

dinner (n)
un dîner
dee-nay

dinosaur (n)
un dinosaure
dee-noh-zor

direction (n)
une direction
dee-rek-syo(n)

directly (adv)
directement
dee-rek-tuh-mah(n)

dirty (adj)
sale
sal

disabled (adj)
handicapé (m)
handicapée (f)
ahn-dee-ka-pay

disco (n)
une discothèque
dee-sko-tek

distance (n)
une distance
dee-stahnss

diving (n)
la plongée
plon-zhay

divorced (adj)
divorcé (m)
divorcée (f)
dee-vor-say

doctor (n)
un médecin
may-duh-sa(n)

dog (n)
un chien
shya(n)

doll (n)
une poupée
poo-pay

dolphin (n)
un dauphin
doh-fa(n)

dome (n)
un dôme
dohm

door (n)
une porte
port

downstairs (adv)
en bas
ah(n) bah

dragon (n)
un dragon
dra-go(n)

dragonfly (n)
une libellule
lee-bel-lewl

drawer (n)
un tiroir
teer-wahr

drawing (act of) (n)
le dessin
de-sa(n)

dream (n)
un rêve
rehv

dress (n)
une robe
rob

drink (n)
une boisson
bwa-so(n)

drinking straw (n)
une paille
pah-ye

drop (n)
une goutte
goot

drugstore (n)
une pharmacie
far-ma-see

drum (n)
un tambour
tahm-boor

drum kit (n)
une batterie
bat-tree

dry (adj)
sec (m) sèche (f)
sek/sehsh

duck (n)
un canard
ka-nar

duckling (n)
un caneton
ka-nuh-to(n)

during (prep)
pendant
pahn-dah(n)

dust (n)
la poussière
poo-syair

duvet (n)
une couette
koo-et

DVD (n)
un DVD
day-vay-day

DVD player (n)
un lecteur de DVD
lek-tuhr duh day-vay-day

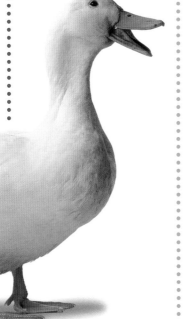
duck
le canard

E

egg
l'œuf

each (adj)
chaque
shak

eagle (n)
un aigle
ay-gluh

ear (n)
une oreille
o-raye

earache (n)
un mal d'oreille
mal do-raye

early (adv)
tôt
toh

earring (n)
une boucle
d'oreille
book-luh do-raye

Earth (planet) (n)
la Terre
tair

earthworm (n)
un ver de terre
vair duh tair

east (n)
l'est (m)
lest

easy (adj)
facile
fa-seel

echo (n)
un écho
ay-ko

edge (n)
le bord
bor

effect (n)
un effet
ay-fay

egg (n)
un œuf
uhf

elbow (n)
un coude
kood

electrical (adj)
électrique
ay-lek-treek

elephant (n)
un éléphant
ay-lay-fah(n)

elevator (n)
un ascenseur
a-sahn-suhr

email (n)
un e-mail
ee-mail

email address (n)
une adresse
électronique
a-dress ay-lek-tro-neek

emergency (n)
une urgence
ewr-zhahnss

empty (adj)
vide
veed

encyclopedia (n)
une encyclopédie
ahn-see-klo-pay-dee

A B C **D E** F G H I J K L M N O P Q R S T U V W X Y Z

end (final part) (n)
la **fin**
fa(n)

English (n)
l'**anglais** (m)
lahn-glay

enough (adj)
assez
a-say

enthusiastic (adj)
enthousiaste
ahn-too-zee-ast

entrance (n)
une **entrée**
ahn-tray

envelope (n)
une **enveloppe**
ahn-vlop

environment (n)
un **environnement**
ahn-vee-ron-mah(n)

equal (adj)
égal (m) **égale** (f)
ay-gal

equator (n)
l'**équateur** (m)
lay-kwa-tuhr

equipment (n)
le **matériel**
ma-tay-ree-el

eraser (n)
une **gomme**
gom

even (adv)
même
mehm

exercise
l'exercice

arm
le bras

hand
la main

envelope
l'enveloppe

Banque Nationale
Champ-de-Mars
Montréal
Québec
H4A 2B8

evening (n)
un **soir**
swahr

event (n)
un **événement**
ay-vayn-mah(n)

every (adj)
tous
too

everybody (pron)
tout le monde
too luh mond

everyday (adv)
tous les jours
too lay zhoor

everything (pron)
tout
too

everywhere (adv)
partout
par-too

exam (n)
un **examen**
eg-za-ma(n)

stamp
le timbre

address
l'adresse

excellent (adj)
excellent (m)
ek-say-lah(n)

excellente (f)
ek-say-lahnt

exchange (n)
un **échange**
ay-shahnzh

excited (adj)
excité (m)
excitée (f)
ek-see-tay

exercise (n)
un **exercice**
ek-sair-seess

exercise book (n)
un **cahier**
ka-yay

exit (n)
la **sortie**
sor-tee

expedition (n)
une **expédition**
ek-spay-dee-syo(n)

expensive (adj)
cher (m) **chère** (f)
shair

experiment (n)
une **expérience**
ek-spay-ree-ahnss

expert (n)
un **expert**
ek-spair

une **experte**
ek-spairt

explorer (n)
un **explorateur**
ek-splor-a-tuhr

une **exploratrice**
ek-splor-a-treess

explosion (n)
une **explosion**
ek-sploh-zyo(n)

extinct (adj)
éteint (m)
ay-ta(n)

éteinte (f)
ay-tant

extra (adj)
supplémentaire
soo-play-mahn-tair

extremely (adv)
extrêmement
ek-streh-muh-mah(n)

eye (n)
un **œil**
uh-ye

eyebrow (n)
un **sourcil**
soor-seel

eyelash (n)
un **cil**
seel

leg
la jambe

foot
le pied

A B C D **E** F G H I J K L M N O P Q R S T U V W X Y Z

F

fashion
la mode

fabulous (adj)
fabuleux (m)
fa-bew-luh
fabuleuse (f)
fa-bew-luhz

face (n)
un visage
vee-zazh

fact (n)
un fait
fay

factory (n)
une usine
ew-zeen

faint (pale) (adj)
faible
fay-bluh

fair (n)
une foire
fwahr

false (adj)
faux (m) fausse (f)
foh/fohss

family (n)
une famille
fa-mee-ye

famous (adj)
célèbre
say-lay-bruh

fantastic (adj)
fantastique
fan-tas-teek

far (adv)
loin
lwa(n)

farm (n)
une ferme
fairm

farmer (n)
un fermier
fairm-yay
une fermière
fairm-yair

fashion (n)
la mode
mod

fashionable (adj)
à la mode
ah la mod

fast (adv)
rapide
rap-eed

fat (adj)
gros (m) grosse (f)
groh/grohss

father (n)
un père
pair

favourite (adj)
préféré (m)
préférée (f)
pray-fair-ay

feather (n)
une plume
plewm

felt pen (n)
un feutre
fuh-truh

female (human) (n)
une femme
fam

fence (n)
une clôture
kloh-tew-ruh

ferry (n)
un traversier
tra-vehr-syah

festival (n)
une fête
feht

field (n)
un champ
shah(m)

field hockey (n)
le hockey
sur gazon
ok-ay soor gah-zo(n)

film (n)
un film
feelm

film star (n)
une vedette
de cinéma
vuh-det duh see-nay-ma

fin (n)
une nageoire
nazh-wahr

fine (adv)
bien
bya(n)

finger (n)
un doigt
dwa

fire (n)
un feu
fuh

fire engine (n)
un camion
de pompier
kam-yo(n) duh pomp-yay

firefighter (n)
un pompier
pomp-yay

first (adv)
d'abord
da-bor

first (adj)
premier (m)
pruhm-yay
première (f)
pruhm-yair

first aid (n)
les premiers
soins
pruhm-yay swa(n)

fish (n)
un poisson
pwa-so(n)

fishing (n)
la pêche
pehsh

fishing boat (n)
un bateau de pêche
ba-toh duh pehsh

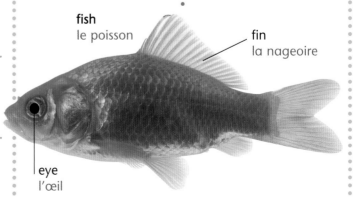

fish
le poisson

fin
la nageoire

eye
l'œil

A B C D E **F** G H I J K L M N O P Q R S T U V W X Y Z

A B C D E **F** G H I J K L M N O P Q R S T U V W X Y Z

fit (adj)
en forme
ah(n) form

flag (n)
un drapeau
dra-poh

flashlight (n)
une lampe de poche
lahmp duh posh

flat (adj)
plat (m) plate (f)
pla/plat

fleece (n)
un polaire
po-lair

flipper (n)
une palme
palm

flock (of sheep) (n)
un troupeau
troo-poh

flood (n)
une inondation
in-on-da-syo(n)

floor (n)
le sol
sol

flour (n)
la farine
far-een

flower (n)
une fleur
fluhr

flute (n)
une flûte
flewt

fly (n)
une mouche
moosh

fog (n)
le brouillard
broo-yar

food (n)
la nourriture
noo-ree-tewr

foot (human) (n)
un pied
pyay

foot (animal) (n)
une patte
pat

foreign (adj)
étranger (m)
ay-trahn-zhay
étrangère (f)
ay-trahn-zhair

forest (n)
une forêt
fo-reh

fork (n)
une fourchette
foor-shet

forward (adv)
en avant
ah(n) av-ah(n)

fox (n)
un renard
ruh-nar

frame (n)
un cadre
kah-druh

free time (n)
le temps libre
tah(n) lee-bruh

freedom (n)
la liberté
lee-bair-tay

freezer (n)
un congélateur
kon-zhay-la-tuhr

French (n)
le français
frahn-say

fresh (adj)
frais (m) fraîche (f)
fray/frehsh

fridge (n)
un réfrigérateur
ray-free-zhair-a-tuhr

friend (n)
un ami, une amie
a-mee

friendly (adj)
amical (m)
amicale (f)
a-mee-kal

fries (n)
les frites
freet

frightened (adj)
effrayé (m)
effrayée (f)
eh-fray-yay

frog (n)
une grenouille
gruh-noo-ye

from (prep)
de
duh

front door (n)
une porte d'entrée
port dahn-tray

fruit (n)
un fruit
frwee

frying pan (n)
une poêle
pwal

fuel (n)
le carburant
kar-bew-rah(n)

full (adj)
plein (m) pleine (f)
pla(n)/plen

fun (n)
un amusement
am-ewz-mah(n)

fun (adj)
rigolo
ree-go-loh

fur (n)
les poils
pwal

furniture (n)
les meubles
muh-bluh

future (n)
l'avenir (m)
lav-neer

frog
la grenouille

G

globe
le globe

game (n)
un jeu
zhuh

garage (n)
un garage
gar-azh

garbage (n)
les ordures
or-dewr

garbage can (n)
une poubelle
poo-bell

garden (n)
un jardin
zhar-da(n)

gardener (n)
un jardinier
zhar-deen-yay

une jardinière
zhar-deen-yair

gardening (n)
le jardinage
zhar-dee-nazh

gas (n)
le gaz
gahz

gas (fuel) (n)
l'essence (f)
le-sahns

gentle (adj)
doux (m) douce (f)
doo/dooss

giant (n)
un géant
zhay-ah(n)

gift (n)
un cadeau
ka-doh

giraffe (n)
une girafe
zhee-raf

girl (n)
une fille
fee-ye

girlfriend (n)
une petite amie
puh-teet a-mee

glass (drink) (n)
un verre
vair

glasses (n)
les lunettes
lew-net

globe (n)
un globe
glob

glove (n)
un gant
gah(n)

glue (n)
la colle
kol

goal (n)
un but
bewt

goat (n)
une chèvre
shay-vruh

God (n)
Dieu
dyuh

gold (n)
l'or (m)
lor

goldfish (n)
un poisson rouge
pwa-so(n) roozh

golf (n)
le golf
golf

good (adj)
bon (m) bonne (f)
bo(n)/bon

gorilla (n)
un gorille
go-ree-ye

government (n)
un gouvernement
goo-vairn-mah(n)

grandfather (n)
un grand-père
grah(n)-pair

grandmother (n)
une grand-mère
grah(n)-mair

grandparents (n)
les grands-parents
grah(n)-par-ah(n)

grape (n)
le raisin
ray-za(n)

grass (n)
l'herbe (f)
lairb

grasshopper (n)
une sauterelle
soht-rel

great (adj)
formidable
for-mee-da-bluh

green (adj)
vert (m) verte (f)
vair/vairt

greenhouse (n)
une serre
sair

ground (n)
la terre
tair

group (n)
un groupe
groop

guide (n)
un guide
gheed

guinea pig (n)
un cochon d'Inde
ko-sho(n) dand

guitar (n)
une guitare
ghee-tar

gymnastics (n)
la gymnastique
zheem-nas-teek

guitar
la guitare

H

habitat (n)
un **habitat**
a-bee-ta

hair (n)
les **cheveux**
shuh-vuh

hairbrush (n)
une **brosse**
à cheveux
bros ah shuh-vuh

hairdresser (n)
un **coiffeur**
kwa-fuhr

une **coiffeuse**
kwa-fuhz

hairy (adj)
poilu (m) poilue (f)
pwa-lew

half (n)
une **moitié**
mwat-yay

hall (n)
un **couloir**
kool-wahr

hamster (n)
un **hamster**
am-stair

hand (n)
une **main**
ma(n)

handkerchief (n)
un **mouchoir**
moosh-wahr

hand towel (n)
une **serviette**
de toilette
sair-vee-et duh twa-let

hang-glider (n)
un **deltaplane**
delta-plan

happy (adj)
content (m)
kon-tah(n)

contente (f)
kon-tahnt

harbour (n)
un **port**
por

hard (adj)
dur (m) dure (f)
dewr

hard drive (n)
un **disque dur**
deesk dewr

hare (n)
un **lièvre**
lyeh-vruh

harvest (n)
une **moisson**
mwa-so(n)

hat (n)
un **chapeau**
sha-poh

hawk (n)
un **faucon**
foh-ko(n)

hay (n)
le **foin**
fwa(n)

he (pron)
il
eel

head (n)
une **tête**
teht

headache (n)
un **mal de tête**
mal duh teht

healthy (adj)
en bonne santé
ah(n) bon sahn-tay

heart (n)
un **cœur**
kuhr

heat (n)
la **chaleur**
sha-luhr

heavy (adj)
lourd (m) lourde (f)
loor/loord

helicopter (n)
un **hélicoptère**
ay-lee-kop-tair

hat
le chapeau

hamster
le hamster

helmet (n)
un **casque**
kask

help (n)
une **aide**
ehd

her/his (adj)
son (m) sa (f)
so(n)/sa

her/him (pron)
la (her) le (him)
l' (before a vowel)
la/luh/l

hero (n)
un **héros**
air-o

heron (n)
un **héron**
air-o(n)

hers/his (pron)
le sien (m)
luh sya(n)

la sienne (f)
la syen

hi
salut
sa-lew

hide-and-seek (n)
cache-cache
kash-kash

high (adj)
haut (m) haute (f)
oh/oht

highway (n)
une autoroute
oh-toh-root

hill (n)
une colline
kol-leen

hip (n)
une hanche
ahnsh

historical (adj)
historique
ee-stor-eek

history (n)
l'histoire (f)
leest-wahr

hive (n)
une ruche
rewsh

hobby (n)
un loisir
lwa-zeer

hockey (n)
le hockey
ok-ay

hole (n)
un trou
troo

holiday (n)
les vacances
vak-ahnss

home (n)
la maison
may-zo(n)

homework (n)
les devoirs
duhv-wahr

honey (n)
le miel
myel

hood (n)
une capuche
kap-ewsh

horn (n)
une corne
korn

horrible (adj)
horrible
o-ree-bluh

horse (n)
un cheval
shuh-val

horseback riding (n)
l'équitation (f)
lay-keet-a-syo(n)

hospital (n)
un hôpital
o-pee-tal

hot (adj)
chaud (m)
shoh
chaude (f)
shohd

hot-air balloon (n)
une montgolfière
mohn-golf-yair

hot chocolate (n)
un chocolat chaud
sho-ko-la shoh

hot dog (n)
un hot-dog
ot-dog

hotel (n)
un hôtel
o-tel

hour (n)
l'heure (f)
luhr

house (n)
une maison
may-zo(n)

how (adv)
comment
ko-mah(n)

huge (adj)
énorme
ay-norm

human (n)
un être humain
eh-truh ew-ma(n)

honey
le miel

hummingbird (n)
un oiseau-mouche
wa-zoh-moosh

hungry (adj)
affamé (m)
affamée (f)
af-fa-may

hurricane (n)
un ouragan
oo-ra-gah(n)

husband (n)
un mari
ma-ree

hut (n)
une cabane
ka-ban

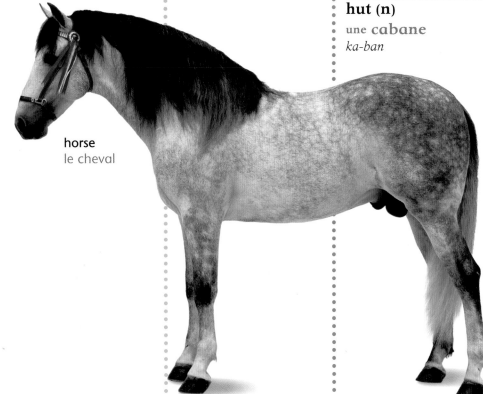
horse
le cheval

A B C D E F G **H** I J K L M N O P Q R S T U V W X Y Z

A B C D E F G H **I** J K L M N O P Q R S T U V W X Y Z

island
l'île

I (pron)
je/j'
zhuh/zh

ice (n)
la glace
glass

ice cream (n)
une crème glacée
krehm glasay

ice cube (n)
un glaçon
glass-o(n)

ice cream
la crème glacée

ice skating (n)
le patinage
sur glace
pa-tee-nazh soor glass

idea (n)
une idée
ee-day

illness (n)
une maladie
ma-la-dee

immediately (adv)
tout de suite
too-duh-sweet

important (adj)
important (m)
am-por-tah(n)
importante (f)
am-por-tahnt

impossible (adj)
impossible
am-po-see-bluh

information (n)
une information
an-for-ma-syo(n)

ingredient (n)
un ingrédient
an-gray-diah(n)

injury (n)
une blessure
bless-ewr

ink (n)
l'encre (f)
lahn-kruh

insect (n)
un insecte
an-sekt

inside (prep)
à l'intérieur de
ah lan-tayr-yuhr duh

instruction (n)
une instruction
an-strewk-syo(n)

instrument (n)
un instrument
an-strew-mah(n)

interesting (adj)
intéressant (m)
an-tair-ay-sah(n)
intéressante (f)
an-tair-ay-sahnt

international (adj)
international (m)
internationale (f)
an-tair-na-syo-nal

Internet (n)
Internet (m)
lin-tair-net

into (prep)
dans
dah(n)

invitation (n)
une invitation
an-vee-ta-syo(n)

iron (clothes) (n)
un fer à repasser
fair ah ruh-pah-say

island (n)
une île
eel

its (adj)
son (m) sa (f)
so(n)/sa

it's (it is)
c'est
say

ice skating
le patinage sur glace

dress
la robe

leg
la jambe

J

jug
la cruche

jacket (n)
un **blouson**
bloo-zo(n)

jam (n)
la **confiture**
kon-fee-tewr

jeans (n)
un **jean**
jeen

jellyfish (n)
une **méduse**
may-dewz

jet (n)
un **avion à réaction**
av-yo(n) ah ray-ak-syo(n)

jewel (n)
un **bijou**
bee-zhoo

jewelry (n)
les **bijoux**
bee-zhoo

job (n)
un **emploi**
am-plwa

joke (n)
une **blague**
blag

journey (n)
un **voyage**
vwa-yazh

judo (n)
le **judo**
zhew-doh

jug (n)
une **cruche**
krewsh

juice (n)
le **jus**
zhew

jungle (n)
la **jungle**
zhahn-gluh

just (adv)
juste
zhewst

jeans
le jean

K

kite
le cerf-volant

kangaroo (n)
un **kangourou**
kahn-goo-roo

karate (n)
le **karaté**
ka-ra-tay

kettle (n)
une **bouilloire**
booy-wahr

key (n)
une **clé**
klay

keyboard (n)
un **clavier**
klav-yay

kind (gentle) (adj)
gentil (m)
zhahn-tee
gentille (f)
zhahn-teeye

kind (type) (n)
une **sorte**
sort

king (n)
un **roi**
rwa

kiss (n)
un **baiser**
bay-zay

kitchen (n)
une **cuisine**
kwee-zeen

kite (n)
un **cerf-volant**
sair-vo-lah(n)

kitten (n)
un **chaton**
sha-to(n)

knee (n)
un **genou**
zhuh-noo

knife (n)
un **couteau**
koo-toh

knight (n)
un **chevalier**
shuh-val-yay

knot (n)
un **nœud**
nuh

koala (n)
un **koala**
ko-a-la

kitten
le chaton

tail
la queue

A
B
C
D
E
F
G
H
I
J
K
L
M
N
O
P
Q
R
S
T
U
V
W
X
Y
Z

A B C D E F G H I J K L M N O P Q R S T U V W X Y Z

L

lemon
le citron

ladder (n)
une **échelle**
ay-shell

ladybug (n)
une **coccinelle**
kok-see-nel

lake (n)
un **lac**
lak

lamb (n)
un **agneau**
an-yoh

lamp (n)
une **lampe**
lahmp

land (n)
un **terrain**
tair-ra(n)

language (n)
une **langue**
lahn-guh

laptop (n)
un **ordinateur**
portable
or-dee-na-tuhr
por-ta-bluh

last (adj)
dernier (m)
dairn-yay

dernière (f)
dairn-yair

late (adv)
en retard
ah(n) ruh-tar

law (n)
une **loi**
lwa

lawn (n)
une **pelouse**
puh-looz

lawn mower (n)
une **tondeuse**
à gazon
ton-duhz ah gah-zo(n)

lazy (adj)
paresseux (m)
pa-re-suh

paresseuse (f)
pa-re-suhz

leaf (n)
une **feuille**
fuh-ye

leather (adj)
en cuir
ah(n) kweer

left (adj)
gauche
gohsh

left-handed (adj)
gaucher (m)
goh-shay

gauchère (f)
goh-shair

leg (n)
une **jambe**
zhahmb

lemon (n)
un **citron**
see-tro(n)

lemonade (n)
une **limonade**
lee-mon-ad

leopard (n)
un **léopard**
lay-o-par

lesson (n)
une **leçon**
le-so(n)

letter (n)
une **lettre**
let-truh

letter carrier (n)
un **facteur**
fak-tuhr

une **factrice**
fak-treess

lettuce (n)
une **laitue**
lay-tew

level (adj)
plat (m) plate (f)
pla/plat

library (n)
une **bibliothèque**
bee-blee-yo-tek

lid (n)
un **couvercle**
koo-vair-kluh

life (n)
la **vie**
vee

lifeboat (n)
un **bateau**
de sauvetage
ba-toh duh sohv-tazh

lifeguard (n)
un **surveillant**
de baignade
soor-vay-ah(n)
duh bayn-yad

life jacket (n)
un **gilet**
de sauvetage
zhee-lay duh sohv-tazh

light (not heavy)
(adj)
léger (m) légère (f)
lay-zhay/lay-zhehr

light (pale) (adj)
clair (m) claire (f)
klair

light (n)
une **lumière**
lewm-yair

lighthouse (n)
un **phare**
far

lightning (n)
un **éclair**
ay-klair

like (prep)
comme
kom

line (n)
une **ligne**
leen-ye

line-up (n)
une **queue**
kuh

lion (n)
un **lion**
lee-yo(n)

liquid (n)
un **liquide**
lee-keed

lizard
le lézard

list (n)
une **liste**
leest

little (adj)
petit (m) petite (f)
puh-tee/puh-teet

living room (n)
un **salon**
sal-o(n)

lizard (n)
un **lézard**
lay-zar

long (adj)
long (m) longue (f)
lo(n)/lon-guh

(a) lot (adj)
beaucoup
boh-koo

loud (adj)
bruyant (m)
brew-yah(n)
bruyante (f)
brew-yahnt

lovely (adj)
adorable
a-do-ra-bluh

low (adj)
bas (m) basse (f)
bah/bahss

lucky (adj)
chanceux (m)
shahn-suh
chanceuse (f)
shahn-suhz

luggage (n)
les **bagages**
bag-azh

lunch (n)
le **déjeuner**
day-zhuh-nay

lunch box (n)
une **boîte-repas**
bwat ruh-pah

tail
la queue

M

mask
le masque

machine (n)
une **machine**
ma-sheen

magazine (n)
un **magazine**
ma-ga-zeen

magician (n)
un **magicien**
ma-zhee-sya(n)
une **magicienne**
ma-zhee-syen

magnet (n)
un **aimant**
eh-mah(n)

magnetic (adj)
magnétique
man-yet-eek

magnifying glass (n)
une **loupe**
loop

mail (n)
la **poste**
post

mailbox (n)
une **boîte aux lettres**
bwat oh let-truh

mailman (n)
un **facteur**
fak-tuhr
une **factrice**
fak-treess

main (adj)
principal (m)
principale (f)
prahn-see-pal

make-up (n)
le **maquillage**
ma-kee-yazh

male (human) (n)
un **homme**
om

mammal (n)
un **mammifère**
ma-mee-fair

man (n)
un **homme**
om

map (n)
une **carte**
kart

marbles (toy) (n)
les **billes**
bee-ye

market (n)
un **marché**
mar-shay

married (adj)
marié (m) mariée (f)
mar-yay

mask (n)
un **masque**
mask

mat (n)
un **petit tapis**
puh-tee ta-pee

match (sport) (n)
un **match**
match

matchbox (n)
une **boîte d'allumettes**
bwat dal-lew-met

math (n)
les **mathématiques**
ma-tay-ma-teek

maybe (adv)
peut-être
puht-eh-truh

me (pron)
me/m' (vowel)
muh/m

meal (n)
un **repas**
ruh-pah

meaning (n)
un **sens**
sahnss

measurement (n)
une **mesure**
muh-zewr

meat (n)
la **viande**
vyahnd

medication (n)
un **médicament**
may-dee-ka-mah(n)

melon
le melon

A B C D E F G H I J K **L M** N O P Q R S T U V W X Y Z

A B C D E F G H I J K L **M** N O P Q R S T U V W X Y Z

milk shake
le lait frappé

melon (n)
un **melon**
muh-lo(n)

menu (n)
la **carte**
kart

mess (n)
le **désordre**
day-zor-druh

message (n)
un **message**
mess-azh

microwave (n)
un **micro-ondes**
mee-kro-ond

middle (n)
le **milieu**
meel-yuh

midnight (n)
minuit
mee-nwee

milk (n)
le **lait**
lay

milk shake (n)
un **lait frappé**
lay frah-pay

million
million
meel-yo(n)

mineral (n)
un **minéral**
mee-nay-ral

minute (n)
une **minute**
mee-newt

mirror (n)
un **miroir**
meer-wahr

mistake (n)
une **erreur**
er-ruhr

mitten (n)
une **mitaine**
mee-tehn

mixture (n)
un **mélange**
may-lahnzh

modelling clay (n)
la **pâte à modeler**
paht ah mod-lay

mom (n)
maman
mah-mah(n)

money (n)
l'**argent (m)**
lar-zhah(n)

monkey (n)
un **singe**
sanzh

monster (n)
un **monstre**
mon-struh

mitten
la mitaine

month (n)
un **mois**
mwa

moon (n)
la **lune**
lewn

more than
plus que
plews kuh

morning (n)
le **matin**
ma-ta(n)

mosque (n)
une **mosquée**
mos-kay

moth (n)
un **papillon de nuit**
pa-pee-yo(n) duh nwee

mother (n)
une **mère**
mair

motor (n)
un **moteur**
mo-tuhr

motorcycle (n)
une **moto**
moh-toh

mountain (n)
une **montagne**
mon-tan-ye

mountain bike (n)
un **vélo**
de montagne
vay-lo duh mon-tan-ye

mouse (animal) (n)
une **souris**
soo-ree

mouse (computer) (n)
une **souris**
soo-ree

mouse pad (n)
un **tapis de souris**
ta-pee duh soo-ree

moustache (n)
une **moustache**
moo-stash

mouth (n)
une **bouche**
boosh

movie theatre (n)
un **cinéma**
see-nay-ma

mud (n)
la **boue**
boo

muddy (adj)
boueux (m)
boo-uh

boueuse (f)
boo-uhz

mug (n)
une **tasse**
tahss

museum (n)
un **musée**
mew-zay

mushroom (n)
un **champignon**
shahm-peen-yo(n)

music (n)
la **musique**
mew-zeek

musician (n)
un **musicien**
mew-zee-sya(n)

une **musicienne**
mew-zee-syen

my (adj)
mon (m) ma (f)
mo(n)/ma

mushroom
le champignon

N

necklace
le collier

nail (n)
un **ongle**
ong-luh

name (n)
un **nom**
no(m)

narrow (adj)
étroit (m) étroite (f)
ay-trwa/ay-trwat

nature (n)
la **nature**
nat-ewr

naughty (adj)
vilain (m)
vee-la(n)

vilaine (f)
veelehn

nest
le nid

near (prep)
près de
preh duh

nearly (adv)
presque
presk

neck (n)
un **cou**
koo

necklace (n)
un **collier**
kol-yay

needle (n)
une **aiguille**
ehg-wee-ye

neighbour (n)
un **voisin**
vwa-za(n)

une **voisine**
vwa-zeen

nephew (n)
un **neveu**
nuh-vuh

nest (n)
un **nid**
nee

net (n)
une **épuisette**
ay-pwee-zet

never (adv)
jamais
zha-may

new (adj)
nouveau (m)
noo-voh

nouvelle (f)
noo-vel

news (n)
les **nouvelles**
noo-vel

newspaper (n)
un **journal**
zhoor-nal

next (adj)
prochain (m)
prosh-a(n)

prochaine (f)
prosh-ehn

nice (adj)
sympathique
sam-pa-teek

niece (n)
une **nièce**
nyehs

night (n)
la **nuit**
nwee

nobody (pron)
personne
pair-son

noisy (adj)
bruyant (m)
brew-yah(n)

bruyante (f)
brew-yahnt

noodles (n)
les **nouilles**
noo-ye

north (n)
le **nord**
nor

nose (n)
un **nez**
nay

note (n)
un **billet**
bee-yay

noodles
les nouilles

notebook (n)
un **carnet**
kar-nay

nothing (n/pron)
rien
rya(n)

now (adv)
maintenant
mehn-tuh-nah(n)

nowhere (adv)
nulle part
newl par

number (n)
un **nombre**
nom-bruh

nurse (n)
une **infirmière**
an-feerm-yair

felt pen
le feutre

notebook
le carnet

A
B
C
D
E
F
G
H
I
J
K
L
M
N
O
P
Q
R
S
T
U
V
W
X
Y
Z

A B C D E F G H I J K L M N O P Q R S T U V W X Y Z

ocean
l'océan

oar (n)
une **rame**
ram

object (n)
un **objet**
ob-zhay

ocean (n)
un **océan**
o-say-ah(n)

office (n)
un **bureau**
bew-roh

often (adv)
souvent
soo-vah(n)

onion
l'oignon

oil (n)
l'**huile (f)**
lweel

old (adj)
vieux (m) vieille (f)
vyuh/vyay

old person (n)
une **personne âgée**
pair-son ah-zhay

Olympic Games (n)
les **Jeux olympiques**
zhuz o-leem-peek

on top of (prep)
sur
soor

onion (n)
un **oignon**
ohn-yo(n)

only (adv)
seulement
suhl-mah(n)

open (adj)
ouvert (m)
oo-vair
ouverte (f)
oo-vairt

opening hours (n)
les **heures
d'ouverture**
uhr doo-vair-tewr

orange juice
le jus d'orange

operation (n)
une **opération**
o-pair-a-syo(n)

opposite (n)
un **contraire**
kon-trair

opposite (prep)
en **face de**
ah(n) fass duh

or (conj)
ou
oo

**orange (colour)
(adj)**
orange
or-ahnzh

orange (fruit) (n)
une **orange**
or-ahnzh

orange juice (n)
un **jus d'orange**
zhew dor-ahnzh

orchestra (n)
un **orchestre**
or-ke-struh

other (adj)
autre
oh-truh

ouch!
aïe !
eye-ye

orange
l'orange

our (adj)
notre (m/f)
no-truh

out of (prep)
hors de
or duh

outside (adv)
dehors
duh-or

oval (n)
un **ovale**
o-val

oven (n)
un **four**
foor

oven mit (n)
un **gant de cuisine**
gah(n) duh kwee-zeen

over there (adv)
là-bas
la-bah

owl (n)
un **hibou**
ee-boo

own (adj)
propre
pro-pruh

owl
le hibou

P

paint can
le pot de peinture

page (n)
une page
pazh

paint (n)
la peinture
pan-tewr

paint brush (n)
un pinceau
pan-soh

paint can (n)
un pot de peinture
poh duh pan-tewr

pair (n)
une paire
pair

palm tree (n)
un palmier
palm-yay

pancake (n)
une crêpe
krehp

panda (n)
un panda
pahn-da

pants (n)
un pantalon
pahn-ta-lo(n)

pantyhose (n)
les collants
ko-lah(n)

paper (n)
le papier
pap-yay

paper clip (n)
un trombone
trom-bon

paper towel (n)
un essuie-tout
es-swee too

parade (n)
un défilé
day-fee-lay

parent (n)
un parent
par-ah(n)

park (n)
un parc
park

parrot (n)
un perroquet
pair-o-kay

part (n)
une partie
par-tee

party (n)
une fête
feht

passenger (n)
un passager
pah-sa-zhay

une passagère
pah-sa-zhair

passport (n)
un passeport
pah-spor

past (history) (n)
le passé
pah-say

past (prep)
après
ap-reh

pasta (n)
les pâtes
paht

path (n)
un chemin
shuh-ma(n)

patient (adj)
patient (m)
pa-sya(n)

patiente (f)
pa-syant

patient (n)
un patient
pa-sya(n)

une patiente
pa-syant

pattern (n)
un motif
mo-teef

paw (n)
une patte
pat

pay (n)
un salaire
sa-lair

pea (n)
un pois
pwa

peace (n)
la paix
pay

pelican
le pélican

pear
la poire

peaceful (adj)
tranquille
trahn-keel

peanut (n)
une cacahuète
ka-ka-weht

pear (n)
une poire
pwahr

pebble (n)
un galet
ga-lay

pedal (n)
une pédale
pay-dal

pelican (n)
un pélican
pay-lee-kah(n)

pen (n)
un stylo
stee-loh

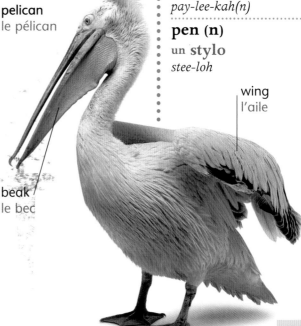

wing
l'aile

beak
le bec

A B C D E F G H I J K L M N O **P** Q R S T U V W X Y Z

pencil (n)
un **crayon à mine**
kray-o(n) ah meen

pencil case (n)
une **trousse**
trooss

penguin (n)
un **manchot**
mahn-shoh

people (n)
les **gens** (pl)
zhah(n)

pepper (n)
le **poivre**
pwa-vruh

perfect (adj)
parfait (m)
par-fay

parfaite (f)
par-feht

perhaps (adv)
peut-être
puh-teh-truh

person (n)
une **personne**
pair-son

pet (n)
un **animal familier**
an-ee-mal fa-meel-yay

phone (n)
un **téléphone**
tay-lay-fon

photo (n)
une **photo**
fo-toh

piano (n)
un **piano**
piano

picnic (n)
un **pique-nique**
peek-neek

picture (n)
une **image**
ee-mazh

piece (n)
un **morceau**
mor-soh

pig (n)
un **cochon**
ko-sho(n)

pine cone
la pomme de pin

pillow (n)
un **oreiller**
o-ray-yay

pilot (n)
un **pilote**
pee-lot

pineapple (n)
un **ananas**
an-an-ass

pine cone (n)
une **pomme de pin**
pom duh pa(n)

pine tree (n)
un **pin**
pa(n)

pink (adj)
rose
rohz

pizza (n)
une **pizza**
peed-za

place (n)
un **endroit**
ahn-drwa

plane (n)
un **avion**
av-yo(n)

planet (n)
une **planète**
plan-eht

plant (n)
une **plante**
plahnt

plastic (adj)
en **plastique**
ah(n) plas-teek

plastic bag (n)
un **sac en plastique**
sak ah(n) plas-teek

plate (n)
une **assiette**
a-syet

play (n)
une **pièce
de théâtre**
pyehs duh tay-a-truh

player (n)
un **joueur**
zhoo-uhr

une **joueuse**
zhoo-uhz

playground (n)
un **terrain de jeu**
tair-ra(n) duh zhuh

playtime (n)
une **récréation**
ray-kray-a-syo(n)

piano
le piano

pine tree
le pin

please (adv)
s'il te plaît
seel tuh pleh

plug (for bath) (n)
un bouchon
boo-sho(n)

plug (electric) (n)
une prise électrique
preez ay-lek-treek

pocket (n)
une poche
posh

pocket money (n)
l'argent de poche (m)
lar-zhah(n) duh posh

point (n)
un point
pwa(n)

polar bear (n)
un ours blanc
oorss blah(n)

pole (post) (n)
un poteau
po-toh

police (n)
la police
po-leess

police car (n)
une voiture
de police
vwa-tewr duh po-leess

**police
helicopter (n)**
un hélicoptère
de police
*ay-lee-kop-tair
duh po-leess*

pond (n)
un étang
ay-tah(n)

poor (adj)
pauvre
poh-vruh

popular (adj)
populaire
po-pew-lair

possible (adj)
possible
po-see-bluh

postal code (n)
un code postal
kohd pos-tal

postcard (n)
une carte postale
kart pos-tal

poster (n)
une affiche
af-feesh

postman (n)
un facteur
fak-tuhr

une factrice
fak-treess

post office (n)
un bureau de poste
bew-roh duh post

potato (n)
une pomme de terre
pom duh tair

pouch (n)
une pochette
po-shet

powder (n)
la poudre
poo-druh

present (n)
un cadeau
ka-doh

president (n)
un président
pray-zee-dah(n)

pretty (adj)
joli (m) jolie (f)
zho-lee

price (n)
un prix
pree

puppet
la marionnette

prince (n)
un prince
pranss

princess (n)
une princesse
pran-sess

prize (n)
un prix
pree

probably (adv)
probablement
pro-bab-luh-mah(n)

problem (n)
un problème
prob-lehm

program (TV) (n)
une émission
ay-mee-syo(n)

project (n)
un projet
pro-zhay

pumpkin (n)
une citrouille
see-troo-ye

pupil (n)
un/une élève
ay-lehv

puppet (n)
une marionnette
mar-yon-net

puppet show (n)
un spectacle
de marionnettes
*spek-tak-luh duh
mar-yon-net*

puppy (n)
un chiot
shyoh

purple (adj)
violet (m) violette (f)
vyo-lay/vyo-let

purse (n)
un sac à main
sak ah ma(n)

puzzle (n)
un casse-tête
kahs-teht

pyjamas (n)
un pyjama
pee-zha-ma

pouch
la pochette

A B C D E F G H I J K L M N O **P** Q R S T U V W X Y Z

81

A B C D E F G H I J K L M N O P **Q R** S T U V W X Y Z

Q R

quarter (n)
un **quart**
kar

queen (n)
une **reine**
rehn

question (n)
une **question**
kest-yo(n)

quickly (adv)
vite
veet

quiet (adj)
silencieux (m)
see-lahn-syuh

silencieuse (f)
see-lahn-syuhz

quietly (adv)
tranquillement
trahn-keel-mah(n)

quiz (n)
un **quiz**
kweez

queen
la reine

racing car
la voiture
de course

rabbit (n)
un **lapin**
lap-a(n)

race (n)
une **course**
koorss

racing car (n)
une **voiture**
de course
vwa-tewr duh koorss

racket (n)
une **raquette**
rak-et

radio (n)
une **radio**
rad-yo

railway station (n)
une **gare**
gar

rain (n)
la **pluie**
plwee

rainbow (n)
un **arc-en-ciel**
ark-ah(n)-syel

raincoat (n)
un **imperméable**
am-pair-may-a-bluh

rainforest (n)
la **forêt tropicale**
for-eh tro-pee-kal

rake (n)
un **râteau**
rah-toh

raspberry (n)
une **framboise**
frahm-bwaz

rat (n)
un **rat**
ra

reading (n)
la **lecture**
lek-tewr

ready (adj)
prêt (m)
preh

prête (f)
preht

real (adj)
réel (m) **réelle** (f)
ray-el

really (adv)
vraiment
vray-mah(n)

receipt (n)
un **ticket de caisse**
tee-kay duh kess

recipe (n)
une **recette**
ruh-set

rectangle (n)
un **rectangle**
rek-tahn-gluh

red (adj)
rouge
roozh

remote control (n)
une **télécommande**
tay-lay-kom-mahnd

report (for school) (n)
un **exposé**
ek-spoh-zay

rescue (n)
les **secours**
suh-koor

restaurant (n)
un **restaurant**
res-tor-ah(n)

rhinoceros (n)
un **rhinocéros**
ree-no-say-ros

ribbon (n)
un **ruban**
rew-bah(n)

rice (n)
le **riz**
ree

rich (adj)
riche
reesh

right (not left) (adj)
droit (m) **droite** (f)
drwa/drwat

right (correct) (adj)
exact (m) **exacte** (f)
eg-zakt

ring (n)
une **bague**
bag

ripe (adj)
mûr (m) mûre (f)
mewr

river (n)
une rivière
reev-yehr

road (n)
une route
root

robot (n)
un robot
ro-boh

rock (n)
un rocher
ro-shay

rocket (n)
une fusée
few-zay

roll (bread) (n)
un petit pain
puh-tee pa(n)

roof (n)
un toit
twa

room (n)
une pièce
pyehs

root (n)
une racine
ra-seen

rope (n)
une corde
cord

rose (n)
une rose
rohz

rough (adj)
rugueux (m)
rew-ghuh

rugueuse (f)
rew-ghuhz

round (adj)
rond (m)
ro(n)

ronde (f)
rond

roundabout (n)
un tourniquet
toor-nee-kay

route (n)
un trajet
tra-zhay

row boat (n)
un canot
kanoh

rubber band (n)
un élastique
ay-la-steek

rug (n)
un tapis
ta-pee

rugby (n)
le rugby
rewg-bee

ruler (measure) (n)
une règle
reh-gluh

running (n)
la course à pied
koorss ah pyay

running shoes (n)
les espadrilles
ehs-pa-dree-ye

S

saddle
la selle

sack (n)
un sac
sak

sad (adj)
triste
treest

saddle (n)
une selle
sel

safe (adj)
en sécurité
ah(n) say-kew-ree-tay

sail (n)
une voile
vwal

sailboat (n)
un bateau à voiles
ba-toh ah vwal

sailor (n)
un marin
mar-a(n)

salad (n)
une salade
sal-ad

sales person (n)
un vendeur
vahn-duhr

une vendeuse
vahn-duhz

salt (n)
le sel
sel

same (adj)
même
mehm

sand (n)
le sable
sah-bluh

sandal (n)
une sandale
sahn-dal

sandcastle (n)
un château
de sable
sha-toh duh sah-bluh

sandwich (n)
un sandwich
sahnd-weetsh

saucepan (n)
une casserole
kass-rol

scarf (n)
un foulard
foo-lahr

school (n)
l'école (f)
lay-kol

school bag (n)
un cartable
kar-ta-bluh

scarf
le foulard

A B C D E F G H I J K L M N O P Q **R** **S** T U V W X Y Z

scissors
les ciseaux

school uniform (n)
un **uniforme**
scolaire
ew-nee-form sko-lair

science (n)
les **sciences**
see-yahnss

scientist (n)
un/une
scientifique
see-yahn-tee-feek

scissors (n)
les **ciseaux**
see-zoh

screen (n)
un **écran**
ay-krah(n)

sea (n)
la **mer**
mair

seagull (n)
une **mouette**
moo-wet

seal (n)
un **phoque**
fok

sea lion (n)
un **lion de mer**
lee-yo(n) duh mair

seaside (n)
le **bord de la mer**
bor duh la mair

season (n)
une **saison**
seh-zo(n)

seaweed (n)
une **algue**
al-guh

second (2nd) (adj)
deuxième
duhz-yehm

seed (n)
une **graine**
grehn

semicircle (n)
un **demi-cercle**
duh-mee sair-kluh

shallow (adj)
peu profond (m)
puh pro-fo(n)

peu profonde (f)
puh pro-fond

shampoo (n)
un **shampooing**
shahm-pwa(n)

shape (n)
une **forme**
form

shark (n)
un **requin**
ruh-ka(n)

sharp (adj)
aigu (m) aiguë (f)
ehg-ew

she (pron)
elle
el

sheep (n)
un **mouton**
moo-to(n)

sheepdog (n)
un **chien de berger**
shya(n) duh bair-zhay

sheet (for bed) (n)
un **drap**
dra

shelf (n)
une **étagère**
ay-ta-zhehr

shell (n)
un **coquillage**
ko-kee-yazh

shiny (adj)
brillant (m)
bree-yah(n)

brillante (f)
bree-yahnt

ship (n)
un **navire**
na-veer

shirt (n)
une **chemise**
shuh-meez

shoe (n)
une **chaussure**
shoh-soor

shopper (n)
un **acheteur**
ash-tuhr

une **acheteuse**
ash-tuhz

shopping (n)
les **courses**
koorss

shopping bag (n)
un **sac**
sak

shopping list (n)
une **liste**
de provisions
leest duh proh-vee-zyo(n)

short (adj)
court (m) courte (f)
koor/koort

shorts (n)
un **short**
short

shoulder (n)
une **épaule**
ay-pohl

show (n)
un **spectacle**
spek-ta-kluh

shower (n)
une **douche**
doosh

shy (adj)
timide
tee-meed

sick (adj)
malade
ma-lad

sidewalk (n)
un **trottoir**
trot-wahr

sign (n)
un **panneau**
pan-noh

silver (n)
l'**argent (m)**
lar-zhah(n)

wool
la laine

sheep
le mouton

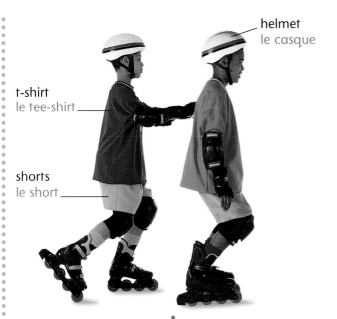

helmet
le casque

t-shirt
le tee-shirt

shorts
le short

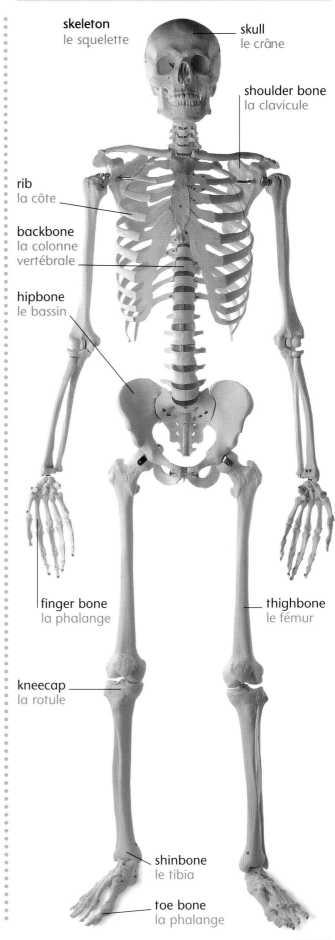

skeleton
le squelette

skull
le crâne

shoulder bone
la clavicule

rib
la côte

backbone
la colonne
vertébrale

hipbone
le bassin

finger bone
la phalange

thighbone
le fémur

kneecap
la rotule

shinbone
le tibia

toe bone
la phalange

simple (adj)
simple
sam-pluh

singing (n)
le **chant**
shah(n)

sink (bathroom) (n)
un **lavabo**
la-va-boh

sink (kitchen) (n)
un **évier**
ayv-yay

sister (n)
une **sœur**
suhr

size (n)
la **taille**
tah-ye

skateboard (n)
une **planche
à roulettes**
plahnsh a roo-leht

skeleton (n)
un **squelette**
skuh-let

skiing (n)
le **ski**
skee

skin (n)
la **peau**
poh

skipping rope (n)
une **corde à sauter**
kord ah soh-tay

skirt (n)
une **jupe**
zhewp

sky (n)
le **ciel**
syel

skyscraper (n)
un **gratte-ciel**
grat-syel

sleeping bag (n)
un **sac de couchage**
sak duh koosh-azh

sleeve (n)
une **manche**
mahnsh

sleigh (n)
un **traîneau**
treh-noh

slipper (n)
une **pantoufle**
pahn-too-fluh

slow (adj)
lent (m) lente (f)
lah(n)/lahnt

A B C D E F G H I J K L M N O P Q R **S** T U V W X Y Z

85

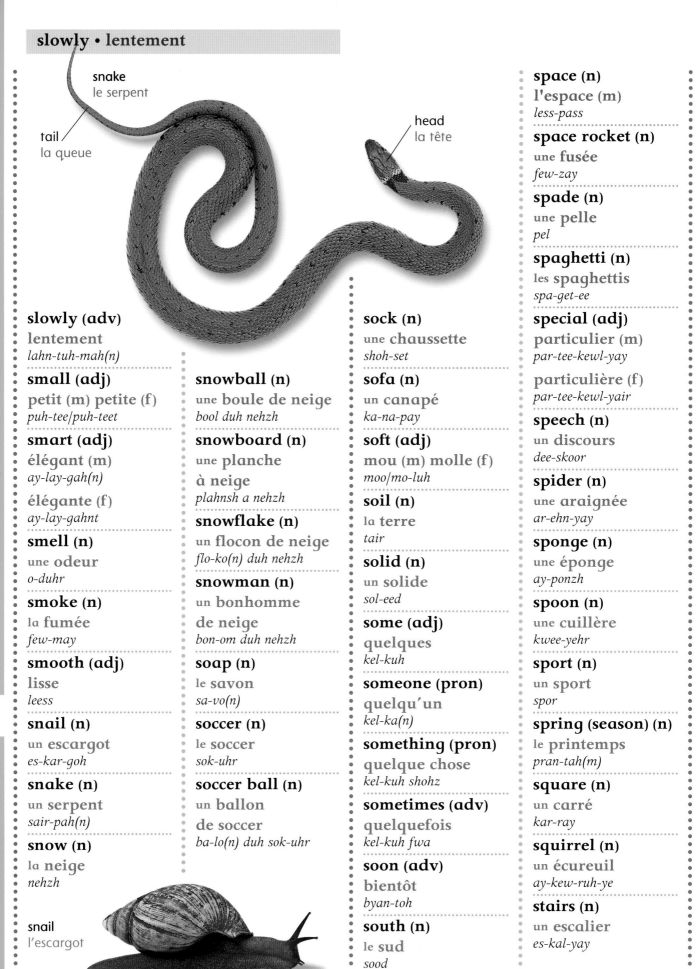

snake
le serpent

tail
la queue

head
la tête

slowly (adv)
lentement
lahn-tuh-mah(n)

small (adj)
petit (m) petite (f)
puh-tee/puh-teet

smart (adj)
élégant (m)
ay-lay-gah(n)
élégante (f)
ay-lay-gahnt

smell (n)
une odeur
o-duhr

smoke (n)
la fumée
few-may

smooth (adj)
lisse
leess

snail (n)
un escargot
es-kar-goh

snake (n)
un serpent
sair-pah(n)

snow (n)
la neige
nehzh

snail
l'escargot

snowball (n)
une boule de neige
bool duh nehzh

snowboard (n)
une planche
à neige
plahnsh a nehzh

snowflake (n)
un flocon de neige
flo-ko(n) duh nehzh

snowman (n)
un bonhomme
de neige
bon-om duh nehzh

soap (n)
le savon
sa-vo(n)

soccer (n)
le soccer
sok-uhr

soccer ball (n)
un ballon
de soccer
ba-lo(n) duh sok-uhr

sock (n)
une chaussette
shoh-set

sofa (n)
un canapé
ka-na-pay

soft (adj)
mou (m) molle (f)
moo/mo-luh

soil (n)
la terre
tair

solid (n)
un solide
sol-eed

some (adj)
quelques
kel-kuh

someone (pron)
quelqu'un
kel-ka(n)

something (pron)
quelque chose
kel-kuh shohz

sometimes (adv)
quelquefois
kel-kuh fwa

soon (adv)
bientôt
byan-toh

south (n)
le sud
sood

space (n)
l'espace (m)
less-pass

space rocket (n)
une fusée
few-zay

spade (n)
une pelle
pel

spaghetti (n)
les spaghettis
spa-get-ee

special (adj)
particulier (m)
par-tee-kewl-yay
particulière (f)
par-tee-kewl-yair

speech (n)
un discours
dee-skoor

spider (n)
une araignée
ar-ehn-yay

sponge (n)
une éponge
ay-ponzh

spoon (n)
une cuillère
kwee-yehr

sport (n)
un sport
spor

spring (season) (n)
le printemps
pran-tah(m)

square (n)
un carré
kar-ray

squirrel (n)
un écureuil
ay-kew-ruh-ye

stairs (n)
un escalier
es-kal-yay

A B C D E F G H I J K L M N O P Q R **S** T U V W X Y Z

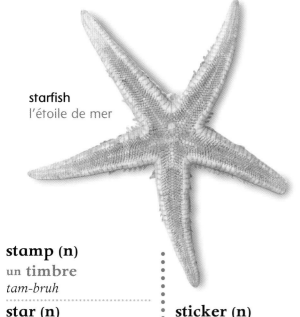

starfish
l'étoile de mer

stamp (n)
un timbre
tam-bruh

star (n)
une étoile
ay-twal

starfish (n)
une étoile de mer
ay-twal duh mair

station (n)
une gare
gar

steam (n)
la buée
bway

steep (adj)
raide
rehd

stem (n)
une tige
teezh

step (n)
un pas
pa

stepfather (n)
un beau-père
boh-pair

stepmother (n)
une belle-mère
bel-mair

stick (n)
un bâton
bah-to(n)

sticker (n)
un autocollant
oh-to-ko-lah(n)

sticky (adj)
collant (m)
ko-lah(n)
collante (f)
ko-lahnt

still (adj)
immobile
im-mob-eel

stocking (n)
un bas
bah

stomach (n)
un estomac
es-to-ma

stone (n)
une pierre
pyair

store (n)
un magasin
ma-ga-za(n)

storey (n)
un étage
ay-tazh

stormy (adj)
orageux (m)
or-azh-uh
orageuse (f)
or-azh-uhz

story (n)
une histoire
eest-wahr

stove (n)
une cuisinière
kwee-zeen-yair

straight (adj)
droit (m) droite (f)
drwa/drwat

strange (adj)
étrange
ay-trahnzh

straw (n)
la paille
pah-ye

strawberry (n)
une fraise
frehz

street (n)
une rue
rew

street light (n)
un réverbère
ray-vair-bair

strict (adj)
sévère
say-vehr

string (n)
une ficelle
fee-sel

stripes (n)
les rayures
ray-ewr

strawberry
la fraise

stroller (n)
une poussette
poo-set

strong (adj)
fort (m) forte (f)
for/fort

student (n)
un/une élève
ay-lehv

stupid (adj)
stupide
stoo-peed

subject (n)
un sujet
soo-zhay

submarine (n)
un sous-marin
soo-ma-ra(n)

subway (n)
un métro
may-troh

suddenly (adv)
tout à coup
toot ah koo

sugar (n)
le sucre
soo-kruh

suit (n)
un costume
kos-tewm

suitcase (n)
une valise
val-eez

summer (n)
l'été (m)
lay-tay

sunflower
le tournesol

A B C D E F G H I J K L M N O P Q R **S** T U V W X Y Z

sun (n)
le soleil
so-laye

sunflower (n)
un tournesol
toor-nuh-sol

sunglasses (n)
les lunettes
de soleil
lew-net duh so-laye

sunhat (n)
un chapeau
de soleil
sha-poh duh so-laye

sunny (adj)
ensoleillé (m)
ensoleillée (f)
ahn-so-lay-yay

sunset (n)
un coucher de soleil
koo-shay duh so-laye

suntan lotion (n)
la crème solaire
krehm so-lair

supermarket (n)
un supermarché
soo-pair-mar-shay

sure (adj)
sûr (m) sûre (f)
soor

surface (n)
une surface
soor-fass

swing
la balançoire

surfboard (n)
une planche de surf
plahnsh duh surf

surfing (n)
le surf
surf

surgery (n)
un chirurgie
shee-ruhr-zhee

surprise (n)
une surprise
soor-preez

surprising (adj)
étonnant (m)
ay-ton-nah(n)

étonnante (f)
ay-ton-nahnt

swan (n)
un cygne
seen-ye

sweater (n)
un chandail
shahn-da-ye

swim goggles (n)
les lunettes de
natation
lew-net duh na-ta-syo(n)

swimming (n)
la natation
na-ta-syo(n)

swimming pool (n)
une piscine
pee-seen

swing (n)
une balançoire
ba-lahn-swahr

T

tadpole
le têtard

table (n)
une table
tab-luh

table tennis (n)
le tennis de table
ten-neess duh tab-luh

tadpole (n)
un têtard
teh-tar

tail (n)
une queue
kuh

tall (adj)
grand (m)
grah(n)

grande (f)
grahnd

tap (faucet) (n)
un robinet
ro-bee-nay

tape measure (n)
un mètre-ruban
meh-truh-rew-bah(n)

taxi (n)
un taxi
tak-see

tea (n)
le thé
tay

teacher (n)
un maître
meh-truh

une maîtresse
meh-tress

team (n)
une équipe
ay-keep

teddy bear (n)
un ours en peluche
oorss ah(n) puh-lewsh

telescope (n)
un télescope
tay-leh-skop

television (n)
la télévision
tay-lay-vee-zyo(n)

tennis (n)
le tennis
ten-neess

tent (n)
une tente
tahnt

term (n)
un mot
moh

terrible (adj)
terrible
tair-ee-bluh

that one (pron)
celui-là
suhl-wee-la

the (article)
le (m) la (f) l'(vowel)
luh/la/l

taxi
le taxi

A B C D E F G H I J K L M N O P Q R **S T** U V W X Y Z

their (adj)
leur (m/f)
luhr

then (conj)
alors
al-or

there (adv)
là
la

thermometer (n)
un thermomètre
tair-mo-meh-truh

they (pron)
ils (m) elles (f)
eel/el

thick (adj)
épais (m) épaisse (f)
ay-pay/ay-pehss

thin (adj)
fin (m) fine (f)
fa(n)/feen

thing (n)
une chose
shohz

third (adj)
troisième
trwaz-yehm

thirsty (adj)
assoiffé (m)
assoiffée (f)
a-swa-fay

this one (pron)
celui-ci
suhl-wee-see

thousand
mille
meel

through (prep)
à travers
ah tra-vair

thumb (n)
un pouce
pooss

thumb tack (n)
une punaise
pew-nehz

thunderstorm (n)
un orage
or-azh

ticket (n)
un billet
bee-yay

tide (n)
la marée
ma-ray

toad
le crapaud

tongue
la langue

tie (n)
une cravate
kra-vat

tiger (n)
un tigre
tee-gruh

tight (adj)
serré (m) serrée (f)
sair-ray

time (n)
l'heure (f)
luhr

timetable (n)
un horaire
or-air

tiny (adj)
minuscule
mee-new-skewl

tire (n)
un pneu
p-nuh

tired (adj)
fatigué (m)
fatiguée (f)
fa-tee-gay

tissues (n)
les papiers-
mouchoirs
pap-yay moosh-wahr

toad (n)
un crapaud
kra-poh

toaster (n)
un grille-pain
gree-ye-pa(n)

today (adv)
aujourd'hui
oh-zhoor-dwee

toe (n)
un orteil
or-teye

together (adv)
ensemble
ahn-sahm-bluh

toilet (n)
les toilettes
twa-let

toilet paper (n)
le papier de
toilette
pap-yay duh twa-let

tomato (n)
une tomate
tom-at

whiskers
les
moustaches

tiger
le tigre

stripes
les rayures

tail
la queue

T

A B C D E F G H I J K L M N O P Q R S T U V W X Y Z

toothbrush
la brosse à dents

tomorrow (adv)
demain
duh-ma(n)

tongue (n)
une langue
lahn-guh

tonight (adv)
cette nuit
set nwee

too (adv)
aussi
oh-see

tool (n)
un outil
oo-tee

tooth (n)
une dent
dah(n)

toothbrush (n)
une brosse à dents
bros ah dah(n)

toothpaste (n)
le dentifrice
dahn-tee-freess

top (n)
le haut
oh

tortoise
la tortue

tornado (n)
une tornade
tor-nad

tortoise (n)
une tortue
tor-tew

toucan (n)
un toucan
too-kah(n)

tough (adj)
dur (m) dure (f)
dewr

tourist (n)
un/une touriste
too-reest

towards (prep)
vers
vair

towel (n)
une serviette
sair-vee-et

town (n)
une ville
veel

toy (n)
un jouet
zhoo-way

toy blocks (n)
les blocs
blok

toy box (n)
un coffre à jouets
kof-fruh ah zhoo-way

tractor (n)
un tracteur
trak-tuhr

traffic (n)
la circulation
seer-kew-lah-syo(n)

traffic lights (n)
les feux de
signalisation
*fuh duh
seen-ya-lee-za-syo(n)*

traffic lights
les feux de signalisation

train (n)
un train
tra(n)

train set (toy) (n)
un train
tra(n)

transport (n)
le transport
trahn-spor

tray (n)
un plateau
pla-toh

tree (n)
un arbre
ar-bruh

triangle (n)
un triangle
tree-yahn-gluh

trip (n)
un voyage
vwa-yazh

tropical (adj)
tropical (m)
tropicale (f)
tro-pee-kal

trouble (n)
un ennui
ahn-wee

trowel (n)
un déplantoir
day-plahnt-wahr

truck (n)
un camion
kam-yo(n)

true (adj)
vrai (m) vraie (f)
vray

trunk (animal) (n)
une trompe
tromp

trunk (tree) (n)
un tronc
tro(n)

T-shirt (n)
un tee-shirt
tee-shirt

tube (n)
un tube
tewb

trunk
la trompe

turkey
le dindon

tummy (n)
un **ventre**
vahn-truh

tunnel (n)
un **tunnel**
tew-nel

tuque (n)
une **tuque**
tew-kuh

turkey (n)
un **dindon**
dan-do(n)

turn (bend) (n)
un **tournant**
toor-nah(n)

turtle (n)
une **tortue de mer**
tor-tew duh mair

twice (adv)
deux fois
duh fwa

twin (n)
un **jumeau**
zhew-moh

une **jumelle**
zhew-mel

U

ugly (adj)
laid (m) laide (f)
lay/lehd

umbrella (rain) (n)
un **parapluie**
pa-ra-plwee

umbrella (sun) (n)
un **parasol**
pa-ra-sol

uncle (n)
un **oncle**
onk-luh

under (prep)
sous
soo

underwear (n)
les **sous-vêtements**
soo-veht-mah(n)

unfair (adj)
injuste
an-zhewst

uniform (n)
un **uniforme**
ew-nee-form

universe (n)
un **univers**
ew-nee-vair

umbrella
le parapluie

uniform
l'uniforme

until (prep)
jusqu'à
zhew-ska

unusual (adj)
inhabituel (m)
inhabituelle (f)
een-ab-ee-tew-el

upside down (adv)
à l'envers
ah lahn-vair

upstairs (adv)
en haut
ah(n) oh

useful (adj)
utile
ew-teel

usually (adv)
d'habitude
da-bee-tewd

V

vacation (n)
les **vacances**
vak-ahnss

van (n)
une **camionnette**
kam-yon-net

vegetable (n)
un **légume**
lay-gewm

vegetarian (n)
un **végétarien**
vay-zhay-ta-rya(n)

une **végétarienne**
vay-zhay-ta-ryen

verb (n)
un **verbe**
vairb

very (adv)
très
treh

vet (n)
un/une **vétérinaire**
vay-tair-ee-nair

video game (n)
un **jeu vidéo**
zhuh vee-day-oh

video player (n)
un **magnétoscope**
man-yay-to-skop

violin (n)
un **violon**
vyo-lo(n)

violin
le violon

W

watering can
l'arrosoir

waist (n)
la **taille**
tah-ye

waiter (n)
un **serveur**
sair-vuh

waitress (n)
une **serveuse**
sair-vuhz

walk (n)
une **promenade**
pro-muh-nad

wall (n)
un **mur**
mewr

wallet (n)
un **porte-monnaie**
port-mo-nay

war (n)
une **guerre**
gair

wardrobe (n)
une **armoire**
arm-wahr

warm (adj)
chaud (m)
chaude (f)
shoh/shohd

warning (n)
un **avertissement**
av-air-tee-smah(n)

**washing
machine (n)**
une **machine
à laver**
ma-sheen ah la-vay

wasp (n)
une **guêpe**
gehp

watch (n)
une **montre**
mon-truh

water (n)
l'**eau** (f)
loh

watering can (n)
un **arrosoir**
ar-rohz-wahr

water lily (n)
un **nénuphar**
nay-new-far

watermelon (n)
un **melon d'eau**
muh-lo(n) doh

wave (n)
une **vague**
vag

we (pron)
nous
noo

weak (adj)
faible
fay-bluh

weather (n)
le **temps**
tah(n)

website (n)
un **site web**
seet web

weed (n)
une **mauvaise
herbe**
moh-vayz airb

week (n)
une **semaine**
suh-mehn

welcome (adj)
bienvenu (m)
bienvenue (f)
byan-vuh-new

well (adj)
bien
bya(n)

west (n)
l'**ouest** (m)
lwest

wet (adj)
mouillé (m)
mouillée (f)
moo-yay

whale (n)
une **baleine**
ba-len

wheat (n)
le **blé**
blay

wheel (n)
une **roue**
roo

wheelbarrow (n)
une **brouette**
broo-et

wheelchair (n)
un **fauteuil roulant**
foh-tuh-ye roo-lah(n)

when (adv)
quand
kah(n)

where (adv)
où
oo

while (conj)
pendant que
pahn-dah(n) kuh

whisker (n)
une **moustache**
moo-stash

whistle (n)
un **sifflement**
see-fluh-mah(n)

white (adj)
blanc (m)
blanche (f)
blah(n)/blahnsh

who (pron)
qui
kee

why (adv)
pourquoi
poor-kwa

wide (adj)
large
larzh

wave
la vague

wing
l'aile

woman (n)
une femme
fam

wood (n)
le bois
bwa

wooden (adj)
en bois
ah(n) bwa

wool (n)
la laine
lehn

word (n)
un mot
moh

world (n)
un monde
mond

worm (n)
un ver
vair

worst (adj)
pire
peer

writing (act of) (n)
l'écriture (f)
lay-kree-tewr

wife (n)
une épouse
ay-pooz

wind (n)
le vent
vah(n)

window (n)
une fenêtre
fuh-neh-truh

windy (adj)
venteux
vahn-tuh

wing (n)
une aile
ehl

winner (n)
un gagnant
gan-yah(n)

une gagnante
gan-yahnt

winter (n)
l'hiver (m)
lee-vair

with (prep)
avec
av-ek

without (prep)
sans
sah(n)

wolf (n)
un loup
loo

Y

yacht
le yacht

Z

zebra
le zèbre

yacht (n)
un yacht
yoht

year (n)
une année
un an (for numbers)
an-nay/ah(n)

yellow (adj)
jaune
zhohn

yesterday (adv)
hier
yair

yogurt (n)
un yogourt
yoh-goor

you (pron)
tu/vous
tew/voo

young (adj)
jeune
zhuhn

your (adj)
votre
vo-truh

zebra (n)
un zèbre
zeh-bruh

zipper (n)
une fermeture éclair
fair-muh-tewr ay-klair

zone (n)
une zone
zohn

zoo (n)
un zoo
zoh

zipper
la fermeture éclair

A
B
C
D
E
F
G
H
I
J
K
L
M
N
O
P
Q
R
S
T
U
V
W
X
Y
Z

French A–Z

In this section, French words are in alphabetical order. They are followed by the English translation and a few letters to show what type of word it is – a noun (n) or adjective (adj), for example. Look at p56 to see a list of the different types of words.

Nouns in French are either masculine or feminine. We have used (m) and (f) to tell you which they are. Sometimes a word in French might mean more than one thing in English, so there might be two translations underneath.

Most of the nouns (naming words) here are singular (only one of the object). To make a noun plural (for more than one thing) you usually just add an "s" – the same as in English. In French though, the other words in the sentence change too – *le* and *la* become *les*. The adjectives also change, usually getting an extra "s" at the end.

à l'arrière (adv)
back (opposite of front)

à l'envers (adv)
upside down

à l'intérieur de (prep)
inside

à la mode (adv)
fashionable

à travers (prep)
through

abeille (n) (f)
bee

absent/absente (adj)
away

accident (n) (m)
accident

acheteur/acheteuse (n) (m/f)
shopper

activité (n) (f)
activity

addition (n) (f)
bill

adorable (adj)
lovely

adresse (n) (f)
address

adresse électronique (n) (f)
email address

adulte (n) (m/f)
adult

aéroport (n) (m)
airport

affaires (n) (f)
business

affamé/affamée (adj)
hungry

affiche (n) (f)
poster

âge (n) (m)
age

agneau (n) (m)
lamb

aide (n) (f)
help

aïe !
ouch!

aigle (n) (m)
eagle

aigu/aiguë (adj)
sharp

aiguille (n) (f)
needle

aile (n) (f)
wing

aimant (n) (m)
magnet

air (n) (m)
air

algue (n) (f)
seaweed

alligator (n) (m)
alligator

alors (conj)
then

alphabet (n) (m)
alphabet

ambulance (n) (f)
ambulance

ami/amie (n) (m/f)
friend

amical/amicale (adj)
friendly

ampoule (n) (f)
bulb (light)

amusement (n) (m)
fun

ananas (n) (m)
pineapple

ancre (n) (f)
anchor

anglais (n) (m)
English

animal (n) (m)
animal

animal familier (n) (m)
pet

année/an (n) (f/m)
year

anniversaire (n) (m)
birthday

antenne (n) (f)
antenna

appareil photo (n) (m)
camera

apparence (n) (f)
appearance

appartement (n) (m)
apartment

après (prep)
after, past

après-midi (n) (m)
afternoon

araignée (n) (f)
spider

arbre (n) (m)
tree

arc-en-ciel (n) (m)
rainbow

arche (n) (f)
arch

B

argent (n) (m)
money, silver

argent de poche (n) (m)
pocket money

armée (n) (f)
army

armoire (n) (f)
wardrobe

arrêt d'autobus (n) (m)
bus stop

arrivée (n) (f)
arrival

arrosoir (n) (m)
watering can

art (n) (m)
art

artiste (n) (m/f)
artist

ascenseur (n) (m)
elevator

assez (adv)
enough

assiette (n) (f)
plate

assistant/assistante (n) (m/f)
assistant

assoiffé/assoiffée (adj)
thirsty

astronaute (n) (m/f)
astronaut

astronome (n) (m/f)
astronomer

athlétisme (n) (m)
athletics

atlas (n) (m)
atlas

au-dessous de (prep)
below

au-dessus de (prep)
above

aujourd'hui (adv)
today

aussi (adv)
also, too

autobus (n) (m)
bus

autocar (n) (m)
coach

autocollant (n) (m)
sticker

automne (n) (m)
autumn

autoroute (n) (f)
highway

autour (prep)
around

autre (adj)
other

avant (prep)
before

avec (prep)
with

avenir (n) (m)
future

aventure (n) (f)
adventure

avertissement (n) (m)
warning

avion (n) (m)
airplane, plane

avion à réaction (n) (m)
jet

avocat (n) (m)
avocado

babouin (n) (m)
baboon

badminton (n) (m)
badminton

bagages (n) (m)
luggage

bague (n) (f)
ring

baignoire (n) (f)
bath

baiser (n) (m)
kiss

balai (n) (m)
broom

balançoire (n) (f)
swing

balcon (n) (m)
balcony

baleine (n) (f)
whale

balle (n) (f)
ball

ballon (n) (m)
ball, balloon

ballon de soccer (n) (m)
soccer ball

banane (n) (f)
banana

banc (n) (m)
bench

bande (n) (f)
band

banque (n) (f)
bank (money)

barbe (n) (f)
beard

barbecue (n) (m)
barbecue

bas/basse (adj)
low

bas (n) (m)
stocking

baseball (n) (m)
baseball

basketball (n) (m)
basketball

bataille (n) (f)
battle

bateau (n) (m)
boat

bateau à voiles (n) (m)
sailboat

bateau de pêche (n) (m)
fishing boat

bateau de sauvetage (n) (m)
lifeboat

bâtiment (n) (m)
building

bâton (n) (m)
bat (sports)

batterie (n) (f)
drum kit

beau/belle (adj)
beautiful

beaucoup (adv)
(a) lot

beau-père (n) (m)
stepfather

beauté (n) (f)
beauty

bébé (n) (m)
baby

bec (n) (m)
beak

belle-mère (n) (f)
stepmother

bête (n) (f)
creature

beurre (n) (m)
butter

bibliothèque (n) (f)
library

bidon (n) (m)
can

bien (adj)
fine

bien (adv)
well

bientôt (adv)
soon

bienvenu/bienvenue (adj)
welcome

bijou (n) (m)
jewel

bijoux (n) (m)
jewelry

billes (n) (f)
marble (toy)

billet (n) (m)
note, ticket

biscuit (n) (m)
cookie

blague (n) (f)
joke

blanc/blanche (adj)
white

blé (n) (m)
wheat

blessure (n) (f)
injury

bleu/bleue (adj)
blue

blocs (n) (m)
toy blocks

blond/blonde (adj)
blonde

blouson (n) (m)
jacket

bois (n) (m)
wood

boisson (n) (f)
drink

boîte (n) (f)
box

boîte aux lettres (n) (f)
mailbox

boîte d'allumettes (n) (f)
matchbox

boîte-repas (n) (f)
lunch box

bol (n) (m)
bowl (cereal)

bon/bonne (adj)
good

bonbon (n) (m)
candy

bondé/bondée (adj)
crowded

bonhomme de neige (n) (m)
snowman

bon marché (adj)
cheap

bord (n) (m)
edge

bord de la mer (n) (m)
seaside

botte (n) (f)
boot

bouche (n) (f)
mouth

bouchon (n) (m)
plug

boucle d'oreille (n) (f)
earring

boue (n) (f)
mud

bouée (n) (f)
buoy

boueux/boueuse (adj)
muddy

bougie (n) (f)
candle

bouilloire (n) (f)
kettle

boulangerie (n) (f)
bakery

boule de neige (n) (f)
snowball

boussole (n) (f)
compass

bouteille (n) (f)
bottle

bouton (n) (m)
button

bracelet (n) (m)
bracelet

branche (n) (f)
branch

bras (n) (m)
arm

brillant/brillante (adj)
bright, shiny

brise (n) (f)
breeze

brosse à cheveux (n) (f)
hairbrush

brosse à dents (n) (f)
toothbrush

brouette (n) (f)
wheelbarrow

brouillard (n) (m)
fog

brun (adj)
brown

bruyant/bruyante (adj)
loud, noisy

buée (n) (f)
steam

buisson (n) (m)
bush

bulbe (n) (m)
bulb (plant)

bulle (n) (f)
bubble

bureau (n) (m)
desk, office

bureau de poste (n) (m)
post office

but (n) (m)
goal

C

c'est
it's (it is)

cabane (n) (f)
hut

cacahuète (n) (f)
peanut

cache-cache (n) (m)
hide-and-seek

cadeau (n) (m)
gift, present

cadre (n) (m)
frame

café (n) (m)
café, coffee

cage (n) (f)
cage

cahier (n) (m)
exercise book

caisse (n) (f)
checkout

calculatrice (n) (f)
calculator

calendrier (n) (m)
calendar

calme (adj)
calm

camion (n) (m)
truck

camion de pompier (n) (m)
fire engine

camionnette (n) (f)
van

campagne (n) (f)
countryside

canapé (n) (m)
sofa

canard (n) (m)
duck

caneton (n) (m)
duckling

canoé (n) (m)
canoe

canot (n) (m)
row boat

cape (n) (f)
cloak

capitale (n) (f)
capital

capuche (n) (f)
hood

carburant (n) (m)
fuel

carnet (n) (m)
notebook

carotte (n) (f)
carrot

carré (n) (m)
square

carrefour (n) (m)
crossing

cartable (n) (m)
school bag

carte (n) (f)
card, map, menu

carte d'anniversaire (n) (f)
birthday card

carte postale (n) (f)
postcard

cartes (n) (f)
cards

carton (n) (m)
cardboard

casque (n) (m)
helmet

casquette (n) (f)
cap

cassé/cassée (adj)
broken

casse-tête (n) (m)
puzzle

casserole (n) (f)
saucepan

cassette (n) (f)
cassette

cave (n) (f)
cellar

CD (n) (m)
CD

ceinture (n) (f)
belt

célèbre (adj)
famous

celui-ci (pron)
this one

celui-là (pron)
that one

centre (n) (m)
centre

cercle (n) (m)
circle

céréale (n) (f)
cereal

cerf-volant (n) (m)
kite

certain/certaine (adj)
certain

cerveau (n) (m)
brain

cette nuit
tonight

chaîne (n) (f)
chain

chaise (n) (f)
chair

chaise longue (n) (f)
deck chair

chaleur (n) (f)
heat

chambre (n) (f)
bedroom

chameau (n) (m)
camel

champ (n) (m)
field

champignon (n) (m)
mushroom

chanceux/chanceuse (adj)
lucky

chandail (n) (m)
sweater

changement (n) (m)
change

chant (n) (m)
singing

chapeau de soleil (n) (m)
sunhat

chaque (adj)
each

chariot d'épicerie (n) (m)
shopping cart

charrette (n) (f)
cart

chat (n) (m)
cat

château de sable (n) (m)
sandcastle

chaton (n) (m)
kitten

chaud/chaude (adj)
hot, warm

chaussette (n) (f)
sock

chaussure (n) (f)
shoe

chauve-souris (n) (f)
bat (animal)

chef (n) (m/f)
chef

chemin (n) (m)
path

cheminée (n) (f)
chimney

chemise (n) (f)
shirt

chemisier (n) (m)
blouse

chenille (n) (f)
caterpillar

cher/chère (adj)
dear, expensive

cheval (n) (m)
horse

chevalier (n) (m)
knight

cheveux (n) (m)
hair

cheville (n) (f)
ankle

chèvre (n) (f)
goat

chevreuil (n) (m)
deer

chien (n) (m)
dog

chien de berger (n) (m)
sheepdog

chimpanzé (n) (m)
chimpanzee

chiot (n) (m)
puppy

chirurgie (n) (f)
surgery

chocolat (n) (m)
chocolate

chocolat chaud (n) (m)
hot chocolate

chose (n) (f)
thing

chou (n) (m)
cabbage

ciel (n) (m)
sky

cil (n) (m)
eyelash

cinéma (n) (m)
movie theatre

cintre (n) (m)
coat hanger

circulation (n) (f)
traffic

cirque (n) (m)
circus

ciseaux (n) (m)
scissors

citron (n) (m)
lemon

citrouille (n) (f)
pumpkin

clair/claire (adj)
clear, light

clavier (n) (m)
keyboard

clé (n) (f)
key

client/cliente (n) (m/f)
customer

cloche (n) (f)
bell

clôture (n) (f)
fence

clown (n) (m)
clown

coccinelle (n) (f)
ladybug

cochon (n) (m)
pig

cochon d'Inde (n) (m)
guinea pig

code postal (n) (m)
postal code

cœur (n) (m)
heart

coffre à jouets (n) (m)
toy box

coiffeur/coiffeuse (n) (m/f)
hairdresser

coin (n) (m)
corner

collant/collante (adj)
sticky

collants (n) (m)
pantyhose

colle (n) (f)
glue

collier (n) (m)
collar, necklace

colline (n) (f)
hill

coloré/colorée (adj)
colourful

comique (n) (m)
comic

commandes (n) (f)
controls

comme (prep)
like

comment (adv)
how

commode (n) (f)
chest of drawers

concert (n) (m)
concert

confiture (n) (f)
jam

confortable (adj)
comfortable

congélateur (n) (m)
freezer

content/contente (adj)
happy

continent (n) (m)
continent

contraire (n) (m)
opposite

coquillage (n) (m)
shell

corde (n) (f)
rope

corde à sauter (n) (f)
skipping rope

corne (n) (f)
horn

corps (n) (m)
body

côte (n) (f)
coast

coton (n) (m)
cotton

cou (n) (m)
neck

coucher de soleil (n) (m)
sunset

coude (n) (m)
elbow

couette (n) (f)
duvet

couleur (n) (f)
colour

couloir (n) (m)
hall

courageux/courageuse (adj)
brave

courbe (adj)
curved

couronne (n) (f)
crown

course (n) (f)
race

course à pied (n) (f)
running

courses (n) (f)
shopping

court/courte (adj)
short

cousin/cousine (n) (m/f)
cousin

coussin (n) (m)
cushion

couteau (n) (m)
knife

couvercle (n) (m)
lid

couverture (n) (f)
blanket

cow-boy (n) (m)
cowboy

crabe (n) (m)
crab

crapaud (n) (m)
toad

cravate (n) (f)
tie

crayon à mine (n) (m)
pencil

crayon de couleur (n) (m)
coloured pencil, crayon

crème (n) (f)
cream

crème glacée (n) (f)
ice cream

crème solaire (n) (f)
suntan lotion

crêpe (n) (f)
pancake

crocodile (n) (m)
crocodile

cruche (n) (f)
jug

cube (n) (m)
cube

cuillère (n) (f)
spoon

cuisine (n) (f)
kitchen

cuisinière (n) (f)
stove

curieux/curieuse (adj)
curious

cygne (n) (m)
swan

D

d'abord (adv)
first

d'habitude (adv)
usually

danger (n) (m)
danger

dangereux/dangereuse
(adj)
dangerous

dans (prep)
into

danseur/danseuse
(n) (m/f)
dancer

danseur/danseuse
de ballet (n) (m/f)
ballet dancer

date (n) (f)
date

dauphin (n) (m)
dolphin

de (prep)
from

de l'autre côté de (prep)
across

dé/dés (n) (m)
dice

décoration (n) (f)
decoration

défi (n) (m)
challenge

défilé (n) (m)
parade

déguisement (n) (m)
costume

dehors (adv)
outside

déjà (adv)
already

déjeuner (n) (m)
lunch

délicieux/délicieuse (adj)
delicious

deltaplane (n) (m)
hang-glider

demain (adv)
tomorrow

demi-cercle (n) (m)
semicircle

dent (n) (f)
tooth

dentifrice (n) (m)
toothpaste

dentiste (n) (m/f)
dentist

déplantoir (n) (m)
trowel

dernier/dernière (adj)
last

derrière (prep)
behind

désert (n) (m)
desert

désordre (n) (m)
mess

dessert (n) (m)
dessert

dessin (n) (m)
drawing (act of)

deux fois
twice

deuxième (adj)
second (2nd)

devoirs (n) (m)
homework

diagramme (n) (m)
diagram

dictionnaire (n) (m)
dictionary

Dieu (n) (m)
God

différent/différente (adj)
different

difficile (adj)
difficult

digital/digitale (adj)
digital

dindon (n) (m)
turkey

dîner (n) (m)
dinner

dinosaure (n) (m)
dinosaur

directement (adv)
directly

direction (n) (f)
direction

discothèque (n) (f)
disco

discours (n) (m)
speech

disque dur (n) (m)
hard drive

distance (n) (f)
distance

divorcé/divorcée (adj)
divorced

doigt (n) (m)
finger

dôme (n) (m)
dome

dos (n) (m)
back (body)

douche (n) (f)
shower

dragon (n) (m)
dragon

drap (n) (m)
sheet (bed)

drapeau (n) (m)
flag

droit/droite (adj)
straight, right (not left)

dur/dure (adj)
hard, tough

DVD (n) (m)
DVD

E

eau (n) (f)
water

échange (n) (m)
exchange

échecs (n) (m)
chess

échelle (n) (f)
ladder

écho (n) (m)
echo

éclair (n) (m)
lightning

école (n) (f)
school

écran (n) (m)
screen

écriture (n) (f)
writing (act of)

écureuil (n) (m)
squirrel

effet (n) (m)
effect

effrayé/effrayée (adj)
frightened

égal/égale (adj)
equal

église (n) (f)
church

élastique (n) (m)
rubber band

électrique (adj)
electrical

élégant/élégante (adj)
smart

éléphant (n) (m)
elephant

élève (n) (m/f)
pupil, student

elle (pron)
she

elles (pron)
they

e-mail (n) (m)
email

émission (n) (f)
program (TV)

emploi (n) (m)
job

en arrière (adv)
backwards

en avant (adv)
forward

en bas (adv)
downstairs

en bois
wooden

en bonne santé
healthy

en colère
angry

en cuir
leather

en espèces
(in) cash

en face de (prep)
opposite

en forme
fit

en haut (adv)
upstairs

en plastique
plastic

en retard
late

en sécurité
safe

encore (adv)
again

encre (n) (f)
ink

encyclopédie (n) (f)
encyclopedia

endroit (n) (m)
place

enfant/enfants (n) (m/f)
child/children

ennui (n) (m)
trouble

ennuyeux/ennuyeuse (adj)
boring

ensemble (adv)
together

ensoleillé/ensoleillée (adj)
sunny

enthousiaste (adj)
enthusiastic

entre (prep)
between

entrée (n) (f)
entrance

enveloppe (n) (f)
envelope

environ (adv)
about

environnement (n) (m)
environment

épais/épaisse (adj)
thick

épaule (n) (f)
shoulder

éponge (n) (f)
sponge

épouse (n) (f)
wife

épuisette (n) (f)
net

équateur (n) (m)
equator

équipage (n) (m)
crew

équipe (n) (f)
team

équitation (n) (f)
horseback riding

erreur (n) (f)
mistake

escalier (n) (m)
stairs

escargot (n) (m)
snail

espace (n) (m)
space

espadrilles (n) (f)
running shoes

essence (n) (f)
gas (fuel)

essuie-tout (n) (m)
paper towel

est (n) (m)
east

estomac (n) (m)
stomach

et (conj)
and

étage (n) (m)
storey

étagère (n) (f)
shelf

étang (n) (m)
pond

été (n) (m)
summer

éteint/éteinte (adj)
extinct

étoile (n) (f)
star

étoile de mer (n) (f)
starfish

étonnant/étonnante (adj)
surprising

étrange (adj)
strange

étranger/étrangère (adj)
foreign

être humain (n) (m)
human

étroit/étroite (adj)
narrow

événement (n) (m)
event

évier (n) (m)
sink (kitchen)

exact/exacte (adj)
right (correct)

examen (n) (m)
exam

excellent/excellente (adj)
excellent

excité/excitée (adj)
excited

exercice (n) (m)
exercise

expédition (n) (f)
expedition

expérience (n) (f)
experiment

expert/experte (n) (m/f)
expert

explorateur/exploratrice (n) (m/f)
explorer

explosion (n) (f)
explosion

exposé (n) (m)
report (for school)

extrêmement (adv)
extremely

F

fabuleux/fabuleuse (adj)
fabulous

facile (adj)
easy

facteur/factrice (n) (m/f)
letter carrier, mailman, postman

faible (adj)
faint (pale), weak

fait (n) (m)
fact

falaise (n) (f)
cliff

famille (n) (f)
family

fantastique (adj)
fantastic

farine (n) (f)
flour

fatigué/fatiguée (adj)
tired

faucon (n) (m)
hawk

fauteuil (n) (m)
armchair

fauteuil roulant (n) (m)
wheelchair

faux/fausse (adj)
false

femme (n) (f)
female (human), woman

fenêtre (n) (f)
window

fer à repasser (n) (m)
iron (clothes)

ferme (n) (f)
farm

fermé/fermée (adj)
closed

fermeture éclair (n) (f)
zipper

fermier/fermière (n) (m/f)
farmer

fête (n) (f)
festival, party

feu (n) (m)
fire

feuille (n) (f)
leaf

feutre (n) (m)
felt pen

feux de signalisation (n) (m)
traffic lights

ficelle (n) (f)
string

fille (n) (f)
daughter, girl

film (n) (m)
film

fin (n) (f)
end (final part)

fin/fine (adj)
thin

flèche (n) (f)
arrow

fleur (n) (f)
flower

flocon de neige (n) (m)
snowflake

flûte (n) (f)
flute

foin (n) (m)
hay

foire (n) (f)
fair

fond (n) (m)
bottom

forêt (n) (f)
forest

forêt tropicale (n) (f)
rainforest

forme (n) (f)
shape

formidable (adj)
great

fort/forte (adj)
strong

foulard (n) (m)
scarf

four (n) (m)
oven

fourchette (n) (f)
fork

fourmi (n) (f)
ant

frais/fraîche (adj)
cool, fresh

fraise (n) (f)
strawberry

framboise (n) (f)
raspberry

français (n) (m)
French

frère (n) (m)
brother

frisé/frisée (adj)
curly

frites (n) (f)
fries

froid/froide (adj)
cold

fromage (n) (m)
cheese

fruit (n) (m)
fruit

fumée (n) (f)
smoke

fusée (n) (f)
rocket, space rocket

G

gagnant/gagnante (n) (m/f)
winner

galet (n) (m)
pebble

gant (n) (m)
glove

gant de cuisine (n) (m)
oven mit

garage (n) (m)
garage

garçon (n) (m)
boy

gare (n) (f)
railway station, station

gâteau (n) (m)
cake

gâteau d'anniversaire (n) (m)
birthday cake

gauche (adj)
left

gaucher/gauchère (adj)
left-handed

gaz (n) (m)
gas

géant (n) (m)
giant

genou (n) (m)
knee

gens (n) (m)
people

gentil/gentille (adj)
kind (gentle)

gilet de sauvetage (n) (m)
life jacket

girafe (n) (f)
giraffe

glace (n) (f)
ice

glaçon (n) (m)
ice cube

globe (n) (m)
globe

golf (n) (m)
golf

gomme (n) (f)
eraser

gomme à macher (n) (f)
chewing gum

gorille (n) (m)
gorilla

goutte (n) (f)
drop

gouvernement (n) (m)
government

graine (n) (f)
seed

grand/grande (adj)
big, tall

grand-mère (n) (f)
grandmother

grand-père (n) (m)
grandfather

grands-parents (n) (m)
grandparents

grange (n) (f)
barn

gratte-ciel (n) (m)
skyscraper

grenier (n) (m)
attic

grenouille (n) (f)
frog

griffe (n) (f)
claw

grille-pain (n) (m)
toaster

gros/grosse (adj)
big, fat

grotte (n) (f)
cave

groupe (n) (m)
group

grue (n) (f)
crane

guépard (n) (m)
cheetah

guêpe (n) (f)
wasp

guerre (n) (f)
war

guide (n) (m)
guide

guitare (n) (f)
guitar

gymnastique (n) (f)
gymnastics

H

habitat (n) (m)
habitat

hamster (n) (m)
hamster

hanche (n) (f)
hip

handicapé/handicapée (adj)
disabled

haricots (n) (m)
beans

haut (n) (m)
top

haut/haute (adj)
high

hélicoptère (n) (m)
helicopter (n)

hélicoptère de police (n) (m)
police helicopter

herbe (n) (f)
grass

héron (n) (m)
heron

héros (n) (m)
hero

heure (n) (f)
hour, time

heures d'ouverture (n) (f)
opening hours

hibou (n) (m)
owl

hier (adv)
yesterday

histoire (n) (f)
history, story

historique (adj)
historical

hiver (n) (m)
winter

hockey (n) (m)
hockey

hockey sur gazon (n) (m)
field hockey

homme (n) (m)
male (human), man

hôpital (n) (m)
hospital

horaire (n) (m)
timetable

horloge (n) (f)
clock

horrible (adj)
horrible

hors de (prep)
out of

hot-dog (n) (m)
hot dog

hôtel (n) (m)
hotel

huile (n) (f)
oil

I

idée (n) (f)
idea

il (pron)
he

île (n) (f)
island

ils/elles (pron)
they

image (n) (f)
picture

immobile (adj)
still

imperméable (n) (m)
raincoat

important/importante (adj)
important

impossible (adj)
impossible

incroyable (adj)
amazing

infirmière (n) (f)
nurse

information (n) (f)
information

ingrédient (n) (m)
ingredient

inhabituel/inhabituelle (adj)
unusual

injuste (adj)
unfair

inondation (n) (f)
flood

insecte (n) (m)
insect

insigne (n) (m)
badge

instruction (n) (f)
instruction

instrument (n) (m)
instrument

intelligent/intelligente (adj)
clever

intéressant/intéressante (adj)
interesting

international/internationale (adj)
international

Internet (n) (m)
Internet

invitation (n) (f)
invitation

J

jamais (adv)
never

jambe (n) (f)
leg

jardin (n) (m)
garden

jardinier/jardinière (n) (m/f)
gardener

jaune (adj)
yellow

je/j' (pron)
I

jean (n) (m)
jeans

jeu (n) (m)
game

jeu de plateau (n) (m)
board game

jeu électronique (n) (m)
computer game

jeu vidéo (n) (m)
video game (n)

jeune (adj)
young

Jeux olympiques (n) (m)
Olympic Games

joli/jolie (adj)
pretty

jouet (n) (m)
toy

joueur/joueuse (n) (m/f)
player

jour (n) (m)
day

journal (n) (m)
diary, newspaper

judo (n) (m)
judo

jumeau/jumelle (n) (m/f)
twin

jumelles (n) (f)
binoculars

jungle (n) (f)
jungle

jupe (n) (f)
skirt

jus (n) (m)
juice

jus d'orange (n) (m)
orange juice

jusqu'à (prep)
until

juste (adj)
correct

juste (adv)
just

K

kangourou (n) (m)
kangaroo

karaté (n) (m)
karate

koala (n) (m)
koala

L

la/lui/l' (pron)
her

là (adv)
there

là-bas (adv)
over there

lac (n) (m)
lake

laid/laide (adj)
ugly

laine (n) (f)
wool

lait (n) (m)
milk

lait frappé (n) (m)
milk shake

laitier/laitière (adj)
dairy

laitue (n) (f)
lettuce

lampe (n) (f)
lamp

lampe de poche (n) (f)
flashlight

langue (n) (f)
language, tongue

lapin (n) (m)
rabbit

large (adj)
wide

lavabo (n) (m)
sink (bathroom)

le/lui/l' (pron)
him

le/la/l'/les (article)
the

le sien/la sienne (pron)
hers / his

leçon (n) (f)
lesson

lecteur de CD (n) (m)
CD player

lecteur de DVD (n) (m)
DVD player

lecture (n) (f)
reading

léger/légère (adj)
light (not heavy)

légume (n) (m)
vegetable

lent/lente (adj)
slow

lentement (adv)
slowly

léopard (n) (m)
leopard

lettre (n) (f)
letter (alphabet, mail)

leur (adj)
their

lézard (n) (m)
lizard

libellule (n) (f)
dragonfly

liberté (n) (f)
freedom

librairie (n) (f)
bookstore

lièvre (n) (m)
hare

ligne (n) (f)
line

limonade (n) (f)
lemonade

lion (n) (m)
lion

lion de mer (n) (m)
sea lion (n)

liquide (n) (m)
liquid (n)

lisse (adj)
smooth

liste (n) (f)
list

liste de provisions (n) (f)
shopping list

lit (n) (m)
bed

livre (n) (m)
book

loi (n) (f)
law

loin (adv)
far

loisir (n) (m)
hobby

long/longue (adj)
long

losange (n) (m)
diamond (shape)

loup (n) (m)
wolf

loupe (n) (f)
magnifying glass

lourd/lourde (adj)
heavy

lumière (n) (f)
light

lune (n) (f)
moon

lunettes (n) (f)
glasses

lunettes de natation (n) (f)
swim goggles

lunettes de soleil (n) (f)
sunglasses

M

machine (n) (f)
machine

machine à laver (n) (f)
washing machine

magasin (n) (m)
store

magazine (n) (m)
magazine

magicien/magicienne (n) (m/f)
magician

magnétique (adj)
magnetic

magnétoscope (n) (m)
video player

maillot de bain (n) (m)
bathing suit

main (n) (f)
hand

maintenant (adv)
now

mais (conj)
but

maison (n) (f)
home, house

maître/maîtresse (n) (m/f)
teacher

mal de tête (n) (m)
headache

mal d'oreille (n) (m)
earache

malade (adj)
sick

maladie (n) (f)
illness

maman (n) (f)
mom

mammifère (n) (m)
mammal

manche (n) (f)
sleeve

manchot (n) (m)
penguin

manteau (n) (m)
coat

maquillage (n) (m)
make-up

marché (n) (m)
market

marée (n) (f)
tide

mari (n) (m)
husband

marié/mariée (adj)
married

marin (n) (m)
sailor

marionnette (n) (f)
puppet

masque (n) (m)
mask

match (n) (m)
match (sport)

matériel (n) (m)
equipment

mathématiques (n) (f)
math

matin (n) (m)
morning

mauvais/mauvaise (adj)
bad

mauvaise herbe (n) (f)
weed

me/moi/m' (pron)
me

médecin (n) (m)
doctor

médicament (n) (m)
medication

méduse (n) (f)
jellyfish

meilleur/meilleure (adj)
better

mélange (n) (m)
mixture

melon (n) (m)
melon

melon d'eau (n) (m)
watermelon

même (adv)
even

même (adj)
same

menton (n) (m)
chin

mer (n) (f)
sea

mère (n) (f)
mother

message (n) (m)
message

mesure (n) (f)
measurement

mètre-ruban (n) (m)
tape measure

métro (n) (m)
subway

meubles (n) (m)
furniture

micro-ondes (n) (m)
microwave

miel (n) (m)
honey

mieux (adj)
best

milieu (n) (m)
middle

mille
thousand

milliard
billion

million
million

minéral (n) (m)
mineral

minuit (n) (m)
midnight

minuscule (adj)
tiny

minute (n) (f)
minute

miroir (n) (m)
mirror

mitaine (n) (f)
mitten

mode (n) (f)
fashion

mois (n) (m)
month

moisson (n) (f)
harvest

moissonneuse-batteuse (n) (f)
combine harvester

moitié (n) (f)
half

mon/ma (adj)
my

monde (n) (m)
world

monstre (n) (m)
monster

montagne (n) (f)
mountain

montgolfière (n) (f)
hot-air balloon

montre (n) (f)
watch

moquette (n) (f)
carpet

morceau (n) (m)
piece

mort/morte (adj)
dead

mosquée (n) (f)
mosque

mot (n) (m)
term, word

moteur (n) (m)
motor

motif (n) (m)
pattern

moto (n) (f)
motorcycle

mou (adj)
soft

mouche (n) (f)
fly

mouchoir (n) (m)
handkerchief

mouette (n) (f)
seagull

mouillé/mouillée (adj)
wet

moustache (n) (f)
moustache, whisker

mouton (n) (m)
sheep

mur (n) (m)
wall

mûr/mûre (adj)
ripe

musée (n) (m)
museum

musicien/musicienne (n) (m/f)
musician

musique (n) (f)
music

N

n'importe qui (pron)
anybody

n'importe quoi (pron)
anything

nageoire (n) (f)
fin

natation (n) (f)
swimming

nature (n) (f)
nature

navire (n) (m)
ship

neige (n) (f)
snow

nénuphar (n) (m)
water lily

neveu (n) (m)
nephew

nez (n) (m)
nose

nid (n) (m)
nest

nièce (n) (f)
niece

Noël (n) (m)
Christmas

nœud (n) (m)
knot

noir/noire (adj)
black

nom (n) (m)
name

nombre (n) (m)
number

nord (n) (m)
north

notre (adj)
our

nouilles (n) (f)
noodles

nourriture (n) (f)
food

nous (pron)
we

nouveau/nouvelle (adj)
new

nouvelles (n) (f)
news

nuage (n) (m)
cloud

nuageux/nuageuse (adj)
cloudy

nuit (n) (f)
night

nulle part (adv)
nowhere

O

objet (n) (m)
object

occupé/occupée (adj)
busy

océan (n) (m)
ocean

odeur (n) (f)
smell

œil (n) (m)
eye

œuf (n) (m)
egg

oignon (n) (m)
onion

oiseau (n) (m)
bird

oiseau-mouche (n) (m)
hummingbird

oncle (n) (m)
uncle

ongle (n) (m)
nail

opération (n) (f)
operation

or (n) (m)
gold

orage (n) (m)
thunderstorm

orageux/orageuse (adj)
stormy

orange (adj)
orange (colour)

orange (n) (f)
orange (fruit)

orchestre (n) (m)
orchestra

ordinateur (n) (m)
computer

ordinateur portable (n) (m)
laptop

ordures (n) (f)
garbage

oreille (n) (f)
ear

oreiller (n) (m)
pillow

orteil (n) (m)
toe

os (n) (m)
bone

ou (conj)
or

où (adv)
where

ouest (n) (m)
west

ouragan (n) (m)
hurricane

ours (n) (m)
bear

ours blanc (n) (m)
polar bear

ours en peluche (n) (m)
teddy bear

outil (n) (m)
tool

ouvert/ouverte (adj)
open

ovale (n) (m)
oval

P

page (n) (f)
page

paille (n) (f)
drinking straw, straw

pain (n) (m)
bread

paire (n) (f)
pair

paix (n) (f)
peace

palme (n) (f)
flipper

palmier (n) (m)
palm tree

panda (n) (m)
panda

panier (n) (m)
basket

panneau (n) (m)
board (notice), sign

pantalon (n) (m)
pants

pantoufle (n) (f)
slipper

papa (n) (m)
dad

papier (n) (m)
paper

papier de toilette (n) (m)
toilet paper

papiers-mouchoirs (n) (m)
tissues

papillon (n) (m)
butterfly

papillon de nuit (n) (m)
moth

pâquerette (n) (f)
daisy

parapluie (n) (m)
umbrella (for rain)

parasol (n) (m)
umbrella (for sun)

parc (n) (m)
park

parce que (conj)
because

parent (n) (m)
parent

paresseux/paresseuse (adj)
lazy

parfait/parfaite (adj)
perfect

particulier/particulière (adj)
special

partie (n) (f)
part

partout (adv)
everywhere

pas (n) (m)
step

passager/passagère (n) (m/f)
passenger

passé (n) (m)
past (history)

passeport (n) (m)
passport

pâte à modeler (n) (f)
modelling clay

pâtes (n) (f)
pasta

patient/patiente (adj)
patient

patient/patiente (n) (m/f)
patient

patinage sur glace (n) (m)
ice skating

patte (n) (f)
foot (animal), paw

pause (n) (f)
break

pauvre (adj)
poor

pays (n) (m)
country

peau (n) (f)
skin

pêche (n) (f)
fishing

pédale (n) (f)
pedal

peigne (n) (m)
comb

peinture (n) (f)
paint

pélican (n) (m)
pelican

pelle (n) (f)
spade

pelouse (n) (f)
lawn

pendant (prep)
during

pendant que (conj)
while

père (n) (m)
father

perle (n) (f)
bead

perroquet (n) (m)
parrot

personne (pron)
nobody

personne (n) (f)
person

personne âgée (n) (f)
old person

petit/petite (adj)
little, small

petit ami (m)
boyfriend

petit-déjeuner (n) (m)
breakfast

petit pain (m)
(bread) roll

petit tapis (m)
mat

petite amie (f)
girlfriend

peu profond/peu profonde (adj)
shallow

peut-être (adv)
maybe, perhaps

phare (n) (m)
lighthouse

pharmacie (n) (f)
drugstore

phoque (n) (m)
seal

photo (n) (f)
photo

piano (n) (m)
piano

pièce (n) (f)
room

pièce de monnaie (n) (f)
coin

pièce de théâtre (n) (f)
play (theatre)

pied (n) (m)
foot

pierre (n) (f)
stone

pile (n) (f)
battery

pilote (n) (m)
pilot

pin (n) (m)
pine tree

pinceau (n) (m)
paint brush

pique-nique (n) (m)
picnic

pire (adj)
worst

piscine (n) (f)
swimming pool

pissenlit (n) (m)
dandelion

pizza (n) (f)
pizza

placard (n) (m)
cupboard

plafond (n) (m)
ceiling

plage (n) (f)
beach

planche à neige (n) (f)
snowboard

planche à roulettes (n) (f)
skateboard

planche de surf (n) (f)
surfboard

planète (n) (f)
planet

plante (n) (f)
plant

plat/plate (adj)
flat, level

plateau (n) (m)
tray

plein/pleine (adj)
full

plongée (n) (f)
diving

pluie (n) (f)
rain

plume (n) (f)
feather

plus que
more than

pneu (n) (m)
tire

poche (n) (f)
pocket

pochette (n) (f)
pouch

poêle (n) (f)
frying pan

poils (n) (m)
fur

poilu/poilue (adj)
hairy

point (n) (m)
point

poire (n) (f)
pear

pois (m)
pea

poisson (n) (m)
fish

poisson rouge (n) (m)
goldfish

poitrine (n) (f)
chest

poivre (n) (m)
pepper

polaire (n) (m)
fleece

police (n) (f)
police

pomme (n) (f)
apple

pomme de pin (n) (f)
pine cone

pomme de terre (n) (f)
potato

pompier (n) (m)
firefighter

pont (n) (m)
bridge, deck (boat)

populaire (adj)
popular

port (n) (m)
harbour

porte (n) (f)
door

porte d'entrée (n) (f)
front door

porte-monnaie (n) (m)
wallet

possible (adj)
possible

poste (n) (f)
mail

pot de peinture (n) (m)
paint can

poteau (n) (m)
pole

poubelle (n) (f)
garbage can

pouce (n) (m)
thumb

poudre (n) (f)
powder

poulet (n) (m)
chicken

poupée (n) (f)
doll

pourquoi (adv)
why

poussette (n) (f)
stroller

poussière (n) (f)
dust

poussin (n) (m)
chick

préféré/préférée (adj)
favourite

premier/première (adj)
first

premiers soins (n) (m)
first aid

près de (prep)
near

président/e (n) (m/f)
president

presque (adv)
almost, nearly

prêt/prête (adj)
ready

prince (n) (m)
prince

princesse (n) (f)
princess

principal/principale (adj)
main

printemps (n) (m)
spring (season)

prise électrique (n) (f)
plug (electric)

prix (n) (m)
price, prize

probablement (adv)
probably

problème (n) (m)
problem

prochain/prochaine (adj)
next

proche (adj)
close (near)

profond/profonde (adj)
deep

projet (n) (m)
project

promenade (n) (f)
walk

propre (adj)
clean, own

prudent/prudente (adj)
careful

punaise (n) (f)
thumb tack

pyjama (n) (m)
pyjamas

Q

quand (adv)
when

quart (n) (m)
quarter

quelque chose (pron)
something

quelquefois (adv)
sometimes

quelques (adj)
some

quelqu'un (pron)
someone

question (n) (f)
question

queue (n) (f)
line-up, tail

qui (pron)
who

quiz (n) (m)
quiz

R

racine (n) (f)
root

radio (n) (f)
radio

raide (adj)
steep

raisin (n) (m)
grape

rame (n) (f)
oar

rapide (adj)
fast

raquette (n) (f)
racket

rat (n) (m)
rat

râteau (n) (m)
rake

rayures (n) (f)
stripes

recette (n) (f)
recipe

récolte (n) (f)
crop

récréation (n) (f)
playtime

rectangle (n) (m)
rectangle

réel/réelle (adj)
real

réfrigérateur (n) (m)
fridge

région (n) (f)
area

règle (n) (f)
ruler (measuring)

reine (n) (f)
queen

renard (n) (m)
fox

repas (n) (m)
meal

réponse (n) (f)
answer

requin (n) (m)
shark

restaurant (n) (m)
restaurant

rêve (n) (m)
dream

réveil (n) (m)
alarm clock

réverbère (n) (m)
street light

rhinocéros (n) (m)
rhinoceros

riche (adj)
rich

rideau (n) (m)
curtain

rien (pron)
nothing

rigolo (adj)
fun

rive (n) (f)
bank (river)

rivière (n) (f)
river

riz (n) (m)
rice

robe (n) (f)
dress

robinet (n) (m)
tap (faucet)

robot (n) (m)
robot

rocher (n) (m)
rock

roi (n) (m)
king

rond/ronde (adj)
round

rose (adj)
pink

rose (n) (f)
rose

roue (n) (f)
wheel

rouge (adj)
red

route (n) (f)
road

ruban (n) (m)
ribbon

ruche (n) (f)
hive

rue (n) (f)
street

rugby (n) (m)
rugby

rugueux/rugueuse (adj)
rough

S

s'il te plaît
please

sable (n) (m)
sand

sac (n) (m)
bag, sack, shopping bag

sac à dos (n) (m)
backpack

sac à main (n) (m)
purse

sac de couchage (n) (m)
sleeping bag

sac en plastique (n) (m)
plastic bag

saison (n) (f)
season

salade (n) (f)
salad

salaire (n) (m)
pay

sale (adj)
dirty

salle à manger (n) (f)
dining room

salle de bains (n) (f)
bathroom

salle de classe (n) (f)
classroom

salon (n) (m)
living room

salut
hi

sandale (n) (f)
sandal

sandwich (n) (m)
sandwich

sang (n) (m)
blood

sans (prep)
without

sauterelle (n) (f)
grasshopper

savon (n) (m)
soap

scarabée (n) (m)
beetle

sciences (n) (f)
science

scientifique (n) (m/f)
scientist

seau (n) (m)
bucket

sec/sèche (adj)
dry

secours (n) (m)
rescue

sel (n) (m)
salt

selle (n) (f)
saddle

semaine (n) (f)
week

sens (n) (m)
meaning

séparément (adv)
apart

serpent (n) (m)
snake

serre (n) (f)
greenhouse

serré/serrée (adj)
tight

serveur (n) (m)
waiter

serveuse (n) (f)
waitress

serviette (n) (f)
towel

serviette de toilette (n) (f)
hand towel

seul/seule (adj)
alone

seulement (adv)
only

sévère (adj)
strict

shampooing (n) (m)
shampoo

short (n) (m)
shorts

sifflement (n) (m)
whistle

silencieux/silencieuse (adj)
quiet

singe (n) (m)
monkey

site web (n) (m)
website

ski (n) (m)
skiing

soccer (n) (m)
soccer

sœur (n) (f)
sister

soir (n) (m)
evening

sol (n) (m)
floor

soleil (n) (m)
sun

solide (n) (m)
solid

sombre (adj)
dark

son/sa (adj)
her/his/its

sorte (n) (f)
kind (type)

sortie (n) (f)
exit

sourcil (n) (m)
eyebrow

sourd/sourde (adj)
deaf

souris (n) (f)
mouse (animal, computer)

sous (prep)
under

sous-marin (n) (m)
submarine

sous-vêtements (n) (m)
underwear

souvent (adv)
often

spaghettis (n) (m)
spaghetti

spectacle (n) (m)
show

sport (n) (m)
sport

squelette (n) (m)
skeleton

stupide (adj)
stupid

stylo (n) (m)
pen

sucre (n) (m)
sugar

sud (n) (m)
south

sujet (n) (m)
subject

supermarché (n) (m)
supermarket

supplémentaire (adj)
extra

sur (prep)
about, on top of

sûr/sûre (adj)
sure

surf (n) (m)
surfing

surface (n) (f)
surface

surprise (n) (f)
surprise

surveillant de baignade (n) (m)
lifeguard

sympathique (adj)
nice

T

table (n) (f)
table

tableau (n) (m)
picture

tableau noir (n) (m)
blackboard

tablier (n) (m)
apron

taille (n) (f)
size, waist

tante (n) (f)
aunt

tapis (n) (m)
rug

tapis de souris (n) (m)
mouse pad

tasse (n) (m)
cup, mug

taxi (n) (m)
taxi

tee-shirt (n) (m)
T-shirt

télécommande (n) (f)
remote control

téléphone (n) (m)
phone (n)

télescope (n) (m)
telescope

télévision (n) (f)
television

temps (n) (m)
weather

temps libre (n) (m)
free time

tennis (n) (m)
tennis

tennis de table (n) (m)
table tennis

tente (n) (f)
tent

terrain (n) (m)
land

terrain de jeu (n) (m)
playground

Terre (n) (f)
Earth (planet)

terre (n) (f)
ground, soil

terrible (adj)
terrible

têtard (n) (m)
tadpole

tête (n) (f)
head

thé (n) (m)
tea

thermomètre (n) (m)
thermometer

ticket de caisse (n) (m)
receipt

tige (n) (f)
stem

tigre (n) (m)
tiger

timbre (n) (m)
stamp

timide (adj)
shy

tiroir (n) (m)
drawer

tissu (n) (m)
cloth

toilettes (n) (f)
toilet

toit (n) (m)
roof

tomate (n) (f)
tomato

tondeuse à gazon (n) (f)
lawn mower

tornade (n) (f)
tornado

tortue (n) (f)
tortoise

tortue de mer (n) (f)
turtle

tôt (adv)
early

toucan (n) (m)
toucan

toujours (adv)
always

touriste (n) (m/f)
tourist

tournant (n) (m)
turn (bend)

tournesol (n) (m)
sunflower

tourniquet (n) (m)
roundabout

tous (adj)
every

tous les jours (adv)
everyday

tout (pron)
everything

tout/toute (adj)
all

tout à coup (adv)
suddenly

tout de suite (adv)
immediately

tout le monde (pron)
everybody

toux (n) (f)
cough

tracteur (n) (m)
tractor

train (n) (m)
train, train set

traîneau (n) (m)
sleigh

trajet (n) (m)
route

tranquille (adj)
peaceful

tranquillement (adv)
quietly

transport (n) (m)
transport

traversier (n) (m)
ferry

très (adv)
very

triangle (n) (m)
triangle

triste (adj)
sad

troisième (adj)
third

trombone (n) (m)
paper clip

trompe (n) (f)
trunk (animal)

tronc (n) (m)
trunk (tree)

tropical/tropicale (adj)
tropical

trottoir (n) (m)
sidewalk

trou (n) (m)
hole

troupeau (n) (m)
flock (of sheep)

trousse (n) (f)
pencil case

tu/vous (pron)
you

tube (n) (m)
tube

tunnel (n) (m)
tunnel

tuque (n) (f)
tuque

U

un/une (article)
a, an

uniforme (n) (m)
uniform

uniforme scolaire (n) (m)
school uniform

univers (n) (m)
universe

urgence (n) (f)
emergency

usine (n) (f)
factory

utile (adj)
useful

V

vacances (n) (f)
holiday, vacation

vache (n) (f)
cow

vague (n) (f)
wave

valise (n) (f)
suitcase

veau (n) (m)
calf

vedette de cinéma (n) (f)
film star

végétarien/végétarienne
(n) (m/f)
vegetarian

vélo (n) (m)
bike

vélo de montagne (n) (m)
mountain bike

vendeur/vendeuse
(n) (m/f)
sales person

vent (n) (m)
wind

venteux
windy

ventre (n) (m)
tummy

ver (n) (m)
worm

ver de terre (n) (m)
earthworm

verbe (n) (m)
verb

verre (n) (m)
glass (drink)

vers (prep)
towards

vert/verte (adj)
green

vêtements (n) (m)
clothes

vétérinaire (n) (m/f)
vet

viande (n) (f)
meat

vide (adj)
empty

vie (n) (f)
life

vieux/vieille (adj)
old

vilain/vilaine (adj)
naughty

ville (n) (f)
city, town

violet/violette (adj)
purple

violon (n) (m)
violin

visage (n) (m)
face

vite (adv)
quickly

voile (n) (f)
sail

voisin/voisine (n) (m/f)
neighbour

voiture (n) (f)
car

voiture de course (n) (f)
racing car

voiture de police (n) (f)
police car

votre (adj)
your

voyage (n) (m)
journey, trip

vrai/vraie (adj)
true

vraiment (adv)
really

Y

yacht (n) (m)
yacht

yogourt (n) (m)
yogurt

Z

zèbre (n) (m)
zebra

zone (n) (f)
zone

zoo (n) (m)
zoo

Speaking French

In this dictionary, we have spelled out each French word in a way that will help you pronounce it. Use this guide to help you understand how the word should sound when you say it. Some French words look the same as English, but sound very different!

Letter	Pronunciation	Our spelling	Example
a, à, â	between the *a* in h*a*t and f*a*r	*a* or *ah*	**adresse** *a-dreys*
ch	like *sh* in *sh*ip	*sh*	**changer** *shahn-zhay*
ç	like *s* in *s*it	*s*	**garçon** *gar-so(n)*
é	like *ay* in d*ay*	*ay*	**café** *ka-fay*
è, ê	like *e* in m*e*t	*eh*	**crème** *krehm*
e	like *er* in oth*er*	*uh*	**de** *duh*
gn	like the *ni* in o*ni*on	*nye*	**ligne** *leen-ye*
i, y	like *ee* in f*ee*t	*ee*	**fille** *fee-ye*
j, and sometimes g	like *s* in mea*s*ure	*zh*	**bonjour** *bon-zhoor*
qu	like *k* in *k*ing	*k*	**queue** *kuh*
o, ô	like *o* in m*o*re	*o* or *oh*	**porte** *port*
r	say *ruh* at the back of your throat, as if you're gargling	*r*	**fleur** *fluhr*
u	like *ew* in f*ew*	*ew*	**tu** *tew*
an, en, ien, in, ain, ein, on, un am, em, im, aim, eim, om, um	the *n* is not pronounced, but the vowel in front of it should have a nasal sound, as if the word ended in *ng*. For example, as if you said *song*, but stopped before saying the final *ng*.	*a(n)*, *ah(n)*, *o(n)*	**bien** *bya(n)*

Verbs

This section gives a list of useful verbs (doing words). You have the infinitive (to...) of the verb. The most useful verbs, such as "to be" *être* and "to have" *avoir*, are written out so that you can see how they change depending on who is doing the action. I = je, you = tu, he/she = il/elle, we = nous, you (plural and formal) = vous, and they = ils/elles.

We have also written out three of the most regular French verbs: to give = *donner*, to finish = *finir* and to sell = *vendre,* so you can see how these change.

There is also a reflexive verb written out. Reflexive verbs are often used where you would say "myself" or "yourself" in English. An example is: to wash oneself = *se laver*.

The verbs that are written out are shown in the present tense – they describe what is happening now.

to act
faire du théâtre
fair dew tay-a-truh

to agree
être d'accord
eh-truh da-kor

to allow
permettre
pair-met-truh

to appear
apparaître
ap-par-eh-truh

to ask
demander
duh-mahn-day

to bake
faire de la pâtisserie
fair duh la paht-eess-ree

to bark
aboyer
ab-wa-yay

to be
être
eh-truh

I am
je suis
you are
tu es
he, she is
il, elle est
we are
nous sommes
you (plural) are
vous êtes
they are
ils, elles sont

to be able
pouvoir
poov-wahr

to be born
être né
eh-truh nay

to be called
être appelé
eh-truh ap-play

to be cold
avoir froid
av-wahr frwa

to be hungry
avoir faim
av-wahr fa(m)

to be scared of
avoir peur de
av-wahr puhr duh

to be thirsty
avoir soif
av-wahr swaf

to become
devenir
duh-vuh-neer

Je fais de la pâtisserie.

Simon croque une pomme.

Elle gonfle un ballon.

114

to close • fermer

Louise **porte** les sacs.

to begin
commencer
kom-ahn-say

to behave
se comporter
suh kom-por-tay

to believe
croire
krwahr

to bend
plier
plee-yay

to bird-watch
observer les oiseaux
ob-zair-vay layz wa-zoh

to bite
croquer
kro-kay

to block
bloquer
blo-kay

to blow
gonfler
gon-flay

to boil
bouillir
boo-yeer

to borrow
emprunter
ahm-pran-tay

to bounce
rebondir
ruh-bon-deer

to brake
freiner
fray-nay

to break
casser
kah-say

to breathe
respirer
ruh-speer-ay

to bring
apporter
ap-por-tay

to brush
brosser
bros-say

to brush one's teeth
se brosser les dents
suh bros-say lay dah(n)

to build
construire
kon-strweer

to bump into
rentrer dans
rahn-tray dah(n)

to buy
acheter
ash-tay

to camp
camper
kahm-pay

to carry
porter
por-tay

to catch
attraper
at-tra-pay

to cause
causer
koh-zay

to celebrate
célébrer
say-lay-bray

to change
changer
shahn-zhay

to charge (a phone)
recharger
ruh-shar-zhay

to check
vérifier
vair-eef-yay

to choose
choisir
shwa-zeer

to clean
nettoyer
net-wa-yay

to clear (a table)
débarrasser
day-bar-ra-say

to climb
grimper
gram-pay

to close
fermer
fair-may

Attrape le ballon !

A B C D E F G H I J K L M N O P Q R S T U V W X Y Z

A B C D E F G H I J K L M N O P Q R S T U V W X Y Z

to collect
collectionner
kol-lek-syo-nay

to come
venir
vuh-neer

to come back
revenir
ruh-vuh-neer

to come from
venir de
vuh-neer duh

to compare
comparer
kom-pa-ray

to complain
se plaindre
suh plan-druh

to contain
contenir
kon-tuh-neer

to continue
continuer
kon-teen-ew-ay

to cook
cuisiner
kwee-zee-nay

to copy
copier
kop-yay

to cost
coûter
koo-tay

to count
compter
kom-tay

to cover
couvrir
koov-reer

to crack
craquer
kra-kay

to crash
s'écraser
say-krah-zay

to create
créer
kray-ay

to cross
traverser
tra-vair-say

to cry
pleurer
pluhr-ay

to cut
couper
koo-pay

to cut out
découper
day-koo-pay

to cycle
faire du vélo
fair dew vay-lo

to dance
danser
dahn-say

to decide
décider
day-see-day

to decorate
décorer
day-ko-ray

to describe
décrire
day-kreer

to destroy
détruire
day-trweer

to die
mourir
moo-reer

to dig
creuser
kruh-zay

*Marie **danse** bien.*

*Caroline **creuse** dans le sable.*

Stéphane jardine.

to disappear
disparaître
dees-par-eh-truh

to discover
découvrir
day-koov-reer

to dive
plonger
plon-jay

to do
faire
fair

I do
je fais
you do
tu fais
he/she does
il/elle fait
we do
nous faisons
you (plural) do
vous faites
they do
ils/elles font

to do the gardening
jardiner
zhar-dee-nay

to draw
dessiner
dess-ee-nay

to dream
rêver
reh-vay

to dress up
s'habiller
sa-bee-yay

to drink
boire
bwahr

to drive
conduire
kon-dweer

to dry
sécher
say-shay

to earn
gagner
gan-yay

to eat
manger
mahn-zhay

to encourage
encourager
ahn-koo-ra-zhay

to enjoy
aimer
eh-may

to escape
s'échapper
say-shap-pay

to explain
expliquer
eks-plee-kay

to explode
exploser
ek-sploh-zay

Je **mange** un gâteau au chocolat.

to face
affronter
af-fron-tay

to fall
tomber
tom-bay

to fall down
s'écrouler
say-kroo-lay

to feed
nourrir
noo-reer

to feel
ressentir
ruh-sahn-teer

to fetch
aller chercher
al-lay shair-shay

to fight
se battre
suh bat-truh

to fill
remplir
rahm-pleer

to find
trouver
troo-vay

to find out
se renseigner sur
suh rahn-sen-yay soor

Il faut **nourrir** les chiens !

A B C D E F G H I J K L M N O P Q R S T U V W X Y Z

A B C D E F G H I J K L M N O P Q R S T U V W X Y Z

to finish
finir
feen-eer

I finish
je finis
you finish
tu finis
he/she finishes
il/elle finit
we finish
nous finissons
you finish
vous finissez
they finish
ils/elles finissent

to float
flotter
flot-tay

to fly
voler
vo-lay

to fold
plier
plee-yay

to follow
suivre
sweev-ruh

to forget
oublier
oo-blee-yay

to freeze
geler
zhuh-lay

to frighten
effrayer
eh-fray-yay

Plie le papier.

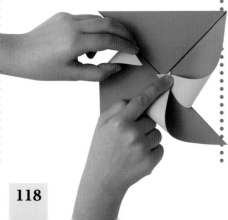

to get
recevoir
ruh-suhv-wahr

to get on (a bus)
monter
mon-tay

to get ready
se préparer
suh pray-pa-ray

to get up
se lever
suh le-vay

to give
donner
don-nay

I give
je donne
you give
tu donnes
he/she gives
il/elle donne
we give
nous donnons
you (plural) give
vous donnez
they give
ils/elles donnent

to go
aller
ah-lay

I go
je vais
you go
tu vas
he/she goes
il/elle va
we go
nous allons
you (plural) go
vous allez
they go
ils/elles vont

to go camping
faire de camping
fair dew kahm-peeng

to go on holiday/ vacation
partir en vacances
par-teer ah(n) vak-ahns

to go out
sortir
sor-teer

to go shopping
faire les courses
fair lay koorss

to grow
pousser
poo-say

to guess
deviner
duh-vee-nay

to hang up (a phone)
raccrocher
rak-ro-shay

to happen
arriver
ar-ree-vay

to hate
détester
day-tes-tay

*Bruno **prend** des œufs pour le petit-déjeuner.*

118

Sophie *s'amuse* !

to have
avoir
av-wahr

I have
j'ai
you have
tu as
he/she has
il/elle a
we have
nous avons
you (plural) have
vous avez
they have
ils/elles ont

to have a shower
prendre une douche
prahn-druh ewn doosh

to have breakfast
prendre le petit-déjeuner
*prahn-druh luh puh-tee
day-zhuh-nay*

to have fun
s'amuser
sam-ew-zay

to have to
devoir
duhv-wahr

to hear
entendre
ahn-tahn-druh

to help
aider
eh-day

to hide
cacher
ka-shay

to hit
frapper
frap-pay

to hold
tenir
tuh-neer

to hop
sauter
soh-tay

to hope
espérer
es-pair-ay

to hurry
se dépêcher
suh day-peh-shay

to hurt
blesser
bless-ay

to imagine
imaginer
ee-ma-zhee-nay

to include
inclure
an-klewr

to inspire
inspirer
an-spee-ray

to invent
inventer
an-vahn-tay

to invite
inviter
an-vee-tay

to join
joindre
zhwan-druh

to jump
sauter
soh-tay

to keep
garder
gar-day

to kick
donner un coup de pied
don-nay a(n) koo duh pyay

to kill
tuer
tew-ay

to kiss
embrasser
ahm-bra-say

to know (someone)
connaître
kon-neh-truh

to know (something)
savoir
sav-wahr

*Les grenouilles **sautent** haut.*

A B C D E F G H I J K L M N O P Q R S T U V W X Y Z

A B C D E F G H I J K L M N O P Q R S T U V W X Y Z

to land (in a plane)
atterrir
at-tair-eer

to last
durer
dew-ray

to laugh
rire
reer

to leap
bondir
bon-deer

to learn
apprendre
ap-prahn-druh

to lie
mentir
mahn-teer

to lift
lever
luh-vay

to like
aimer
eh-may

to listen to
écouter
ay-koo-tay

to live
vivre
veev-ruh

to lock
fermer à clé
fair-may ah klay

to look
regarder
ruh-gar-day

to look after
s'occuper de
sok-ew-pay duh

to look for
chercher
shair-shay

to lose
perdre
pair-druh

to love
aimer
eh-may

to magnify
grossir
groh-seer

to make
fabriquer
fab-ree-kay

to make a wish
faire un vœu
fair a(n) vuh

to make friends
se faire des amis
suh fair dez a-mee

to marry
se marier
suh mar-yay

to mean
signifier
seen-yeef-yay

to meet
rencontrer
rahn-kon-tray

to move
bouger
boo-zhay

to need
avoir besoin de
av-wahr buh-zwah(n) duh

to not feel well
ne pas se sentir bien
nuh pah suh sahn-teer bya(n)

to notice
remarquer
ruh-mar-kay

to offer
offrir
off-reer

to open
ouvrir
oov-reer

to own
posséder
po-say-day

Lucie ouvre la porte.

Philippe écoute de la musique.

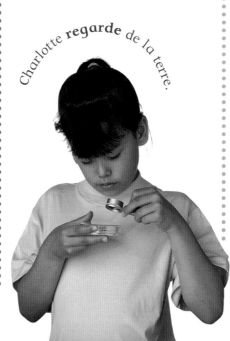

Charlotte regarde de la terre.

120

to pack
faire les valises
fair lay val-eez

to paint
peindre
pan-druh

to pay
payer
pay-yay

to persuade
persuader
pair-swa-day

to pick up
ramasser
ram-ah-say

to plan
organiser
or-gan-ee-zay

to play
jouer
zhoo-ay

to play an instrument
jouer d'un instrument
zhoo-ay dune ahn-stre-mahn

to point
indiquer
an-dee-kay

to pour
verser
vair-say

to practise
s'entraîner
sahn-treh-nay

to predict
prédire
pray-deer

to prefer
préférer
pray-fair-ay

to prepare
préparer
pray-pa-ray

to press
appuyer sur
ap-pwee-yay soor

to pretend
faire semblant
fair sahm-blah(n)

to print
imprimer
am-pree-may

to produce
produire
pro-dweer

to promise
promettre
pro-met-truh

to protect
protéger
pro-tay-zhay

to provide
fournir
foor-neer

to pull
tirer
teer-ay

to push
pousser
poo-say

to put
mettre
met-truh

to put away
ranger
rahn-zhay

to rain
pleuvoir
pluhv-wahr

to reach
atteindre
at-tan-druh

Verse l'eau doucement !

Peux-tu peindre un tableau ?

A B C D E F G H I J K L M N O P Q R S T U V W X Y Z

A B C D E F G H I J K L M N O P Q R S T U V W X Y Z

to read
lire
leer

to realize
se rendre compte
suh rahn-druh komt

to recognize
reconnaître
ruh-kon-neh-truh

to refuse
refuser
ruh-few-zay

to relax
se détendre
suh day-tahn-druh

to remain
rester
res-tay

to remember
se souvenir de
suh soo-vuh-neer duh

to repair
réparer
ray-pa-ray

to rest
se reposer
suh ruh-poh-zay

to return
revenir
ruh-vuh-neer

Mathieu **court** vite.

to ride a bike
faire du vélo
fair dew vay-lo

to ride a horse
monter à cheval
mon-tay ah shuh-val

to ring
sonner
so-nay

to roll
rouler
roo-lay

to rollerblade
faire du patin en ligne
fair dew pa-ta(n) ah(n) leen-ye

to row
ramer
ra-may

to rub
frotter
fro-tay

to run
courir
koo-reer

to run after
poursuivre
poor-swee-vruh

to sail
faire de la voile
fair duh la vwal

to save
sauver
soh-vay

to say
dire
deer

to score (a goal)
marquer
mar-kay

to scratch (oneself)
se gratter
suh grat-tay

to search
chercher
shair-shay

to see
voir
vwahr

to seem
sembler
sahm-blay

Mélanie **monte** à cheval.

Julie **lit** son livre.

to sell
vendre
vahn-druh

I sell
je vends
you sell
tu vends
he/she sells
il/elle vend
we sell
nous vendons
you (plural) sell
vous vendez
they sell
ils/elles vendent

to send
envoyer
ahn-vwa-yay

to set a table
mettre la table
met-truh la tab-luh

to share
partager
par-ta-zhay

to shine
briller
bree-yay

to shout
crier
kree-yay

Léa **crie** après son amie.

Clément **dort**.

to show
montrer
mon-tray

to sing
chanter
shahn-tay

to sit
s'asseoir
sass-wahr

to skate (on ice)
patiner (sur glace)
pa-tee-nay

to ski
skier
skee-yay

to sleep
dormir
dor-meer

to slide
glisser
glee-say

to slip
glisser
glee-say

to smell
sentir
sahn-teer

to smile
sourire
soo-reer

to snow
neiger
nay-zhay

to sound (like)
sembler
sahm-blay

to speak
parler
par-lay

to spell
épeler
ay-puh-lay

to spin
tourner
toor-nay

to spread
étaler
ay-ta-lay

to stand
se tenir debout
suh tuh-neer duh-boo

to stand up
se lever
suh luh-vay

to start
commencer
kom-ahn-say

to stay
rester
res-tay

to stick
coller
kol-lay

Étale le chocolat sur les gâteaux.

A B C D E F G H I J K L M N O P Q R S T U V W X Y Z

123

A B C D E F G H I J K L M N O P Q R S T U V W X Y Z

to sting • piquer

La fille prend une photo.

to sting
piquer
pee-kay

to stop
arrêter
arh-reh-tay

to stretch
s'étirer
say-teer-ay

to study
étudier
ay-tewd-yay

to surf
surfer
soor-fay

to surprise
surprendre
soor-prahn-druh

to survive
survivre
soor-veev-ruh

to swim
nager
na-zhay

to take
prendre
prahn-druh

to take a photo
prendre une photo
prahn-druh ewn fo-toh

to take away
emporter
ahm-por-tay

to take turns
faire à tour de rôle
fair ah toor duh rohl

to talk
parler
par-lay

to taste
goûter
goo-tay

to teach
enseigner
ahn-sen-yay

to tease
taquiner
tak-ee-nay

to tell
raconter
rak-on-tay

to tell a story
raconter une histoire
rak-on-tay ewn eest-wahr

to tell the time
dire l'heure
deer luhr

to thank
remercier
ruh-mair-syay

to think
réfléchir
ray-flay-sheer

Valérie réfléchit.

to throw
jeter
zhuh-tay

to tidy up
ranger
rahn-zhay

to tie
attacher
at-ta-shay

to touch
toucher
too-shay

to train
entraîner
ahn-treh-nay

to translate
traduire
trad-weer

to travel
voyager
vwa-ya-zhay

to treat (well)
traiter (bien)
tray-tay bya(n)

to try (on)
essayer
es-say-yay

to turn
tourner
toor-nay

Jean s'entraîne.

124